Staunin Ma Lane

Staunin Ma Lane

獨立

Chinese Verse in Scots and English

Owreset bi

Brian Holton

霍布恩

Shearsman Books

First published in the United Kingdom in 2016 by
Shearsman Books
50 Westons Hill Drive
Emersons Green
BRISTOL
BS16 7DF

Shearsman Books Ltd Registered Office
30–31 St. James Place, Mangotsfield, Bristol BS16 9JB
(this address not for correspondence)

www.shearsman.com

ISBN 978-1-84861-466-6

TRANSLATOR'S ACKNOWLEDGEMENTS
The translator would like to thank Helen Douglas and Telfer Stokes for *Water on the Border*, John Minford for
his support as well as for *A Birthday Book for Brother Stone*, John Law at *Lallans* for *The Nine Sangs*, Ted Huters
at *Renditions* for *Du Fu: A Poem and a Provocation*, Alec Finlay, Peter Kravitz, Murdo Macdonald, Glenn Murray,
Joy Hendry, Tommy McClellan, Stuart McHardy, John Cayley and Bill Herbert for their enthusiasm and
encouragement, Tony Frazer for taking on such an improbable project and making such a beautiful book of it,
and Monika Holton for starting the whole thing off.

NOTE TO THE READER
I have provided no glossary for non-Scots speaking readers, as the magisterial fruit of
many generations of scholarship that is the *Dictionar o the Scots Leid* is available free at
www.dsl.ac.uk.

Contents

Owre monie's the nation an monie's the sea wis A cairriet
for ti win hame ti thae wanhairtsome obsequies, oh ma brither,
sae's A micht ser ye the solemn sepulchrals for the defunct
and uiselessly speak ma piece ti the dumb aiss at's left o ye,
for wickit weird hes reivit yir livin sel frae me.
Ochone, ma puir brither, tint ti me nou sae unglaidlie,
tak ye nou thae things, the wey our langsyne fore-elders
haunit doun ti us, set out in wanhappy exequies;
tak ye tae, aathegither droukit wi a brither's tears,
ma halse, brither, an ma fareweill for ever mair.

Catullus 101

Prelude
楔子

Water on the Border
邊疆水

These poems were commissioned by artists Helen Douglas and Telfer Stokes for their lovely art book *Water on the Border* (Yarrow: Weproductions 1994): in it, they present their art with drawings by schoolchildren in Yarrow, Scottish Borders, and in Hangzhou, China, all made in response to the same set of Chinese poems which share the theme of water or the waterside. I translated these for the artists, and I present them here shorn of their beautiful context. I have made minor revisions to the published versions.

Li Bai   701-762

Frae the Hairt, Fou in Springtime

This warld's like ae muckle dream:
whit for wad ye trauchle yir life awa?
Liefer stey on the batter aa yir days,
an dover easie-ozie ben the hous.
A wakent, and spied on the green,
in amang the flouers, a wheeplin bird:
"Whit day's it the day?" speirs A,
an on the spring wind cam the merle's sang.
Great o hairt, A gied a lang souch,
turnt an poured masel anither dram;
A sang a rant, waitin on the mune,
an forgot aa else yince it wis sung.

李 白

Li Bai

春日醉起言志

From the Heart, Drunk in Springtime

處世若大夢
胡為勞其生
所以終日醉
頹然臥前楹
覺來眄庭前
一鳥花間鳴
借問此何時
春風語流鶯
感之欲嘆息
對酒還自傾
浩歌待明月
曲盡已忘情

This world is like one huge dream:
why should you toil your life away?
Better to stay drunk all your days
and doze at home in idleness.
I woke and saw on the grass,
among the flowers, a whistling bird.
"What day is it?" I asked,
and on the spring wind came the blackbird's[1] song.
Heavy of heart, I turned and poured myself a drink:
I sang a ranting song, waiting for the moon,
and forgot all else once I'd sung it.

---

[1] Naturalised: *oriole* in the original.

Tao Yuanming (365-427)　　　　　　陶淵明

Hingin Clouds　　　　　　　　　停雲

Hingin clouds rowin, rowin,　　　　靄靄停雲
timeous rain drowie, drowie,　　　　蒙蒙時雨
mirk an mirk in ilka airt,　　　　　八表同昏
haughs turnt aa ti rivers.　　　　　平路伊阻
There's drink, there's drink,　　　　有酒有酒
ti cannily tak at the eastren windae,　閑飲東窗
thinkin lang, wearyin on ma freins,　願言懷人
naither cairt nor coble comin near uis.　舟車靡從

Low Cloud

Low clouds rolling, rolling;
seasonal rain drizzling, drizzling;
dark, dark in every direction,
riverbanks all broken.
There's drink, there's drink
to sip quietly at the eastern window,
thinking long, yearning for my friends,
neither carriage nor boat coming near me.

Qiwu Qian 692-c749   綦毋潛

Driftin on Ruoye Watter in the Spring   春泛若耶溪

There's nae en to wearyin for easedom:
frae here, A'll wander whaur A will.
The gloaming wind 'll blaw ma boatie on
intae the watter-fuit's flouerie yett.
Nicht faas, an A turn to the westlin corries:
A watch the staurs outowre the braes;
a gowstie haar gaes fleein abune the stank;
ahint the wuids, a laich mune faas.
Life's but a muckle watter in spate –
oh, gin A wis a cantie fisher-lad!

幽意無斷絕
此去隨所偶
晚風吹行舟
花路入溪口
際夜轉西壑
隔山望南斗
潭煙飛溶溶
林月低向后
生事且彌漫
願為持竿叟

Drifting on Ruoye River in the Spring

There's no end to longing for ease:
from here, I'm going to wander at will.
The evening wind will blow my little boat onward,
into the flowery gate of the river mouth.
Night falls, and I turn to the western corries:
I watch the stars out beyond the slopes;
a gust blows the mists away above the pool;
behind the woods a low moon sets.
Life's but a huge river in spate –
oh to be a happy fisher-boy!

Li Bai (701-762)

Bouzin Ma Lane Ablow the Mune

Amang the flouers wi a pig o whisky,
boozin ma lane, wi ne'er a frein,
A lift ma gless ti cry the mune in:
ma sheddae, the mune, and me maks thrie.
The mune's nae great boozer, tho,
an ma sheddae juist follaes uis about:
an inconstant cronie, a mune-sheddae,
but sprees in springtime there maun be.
Gin A sing, the mune shoogles back an forrit;
gin A dance, ma sheddae stotters aa aroun:
whan we're whiskified we're blithe thegither
but gin we sober up we'll hae ti pairt –
sae we'll ramble an rant on forever
gallivantin thegither the galaxie owre!

李 白

Li Bai

月下獨酌
其一

Boozing Alone Under the Moon

花間一壺酒
酌無相親
舉杯邀明月
對影成三人
月既不解飲
影徒隨我身
暫伴月將影
行樂須及春
我歌月徘徊
我舞影零亂
醒時同交歡
醉后各分散
永結無情游
相期邈雲漢

Among the flowers with a jug of wine,
　　boozing alone, without a friend,
I lift my glass to invite the moon in:
　my shadow, the moon, and me makes three.
　The moon's no great boozer, though,
　and my shadow just follows me around:
　　an inconstant crony, a moon-shadow,
　but there have to be sprees in springtime.
If I sing, the moon sways unsteadily back and forward;
　if I dance, my shadow staggers all over:
　when we're liquored up, we're happy together,
　　but if we sober up we'll have to part –
　so we'll ramble on and carouse forever,
　gallivanting together across the galaxy!

Zhang Xiaoxiang (1132-1169)

Whit a Nicht!
Ti the air *Lillie Leesome Niannu*

On the gress-green lochs o Dongting
nearhaun mid-hairst,
no a braith o wind:
a field o jade, a jewelt warld acres wide,
whaur ma coble's a wee soumin leaf.
Twae munes leam,
twae siller galaxies shine,
skimmerin bricht, ablow an abune.
The hairt 'll easy read sic messages,
but the ferlie o't A canna weill tell ye, sir.
A bude ti mind on thae lang years southawa
whan, bi the licht o ma aefauld hairt's leam,
brichter nor the snaa wis ma lealty.
Tho A'm scrimp o the pow, and A'm chitterin wi the cauld,
A'll drift a whylie yet on caller waters, cairrie-braid.
The haill Westlan Watter's pourin out here
for me ti ladle't aa inti the staurs o the Pleuch,
an staun a roun for aa Creation!
Clappin on the rimwale, singin ti masel –
Whit a nicht! Whit a nicht!

張孝祥

念奴娇·過洞庭

洞庭青草
近中秋
更無一點風色
玉鑒瓊田三萬頃
著我扁舟一葉
素月分輝
明河共影
表里俱澄澈
悠然心會
妙處難與君說
應念嶺表經年
孤光自照
肝膽皆冰雪
短髮蕭疏襟袖冷
穩泛滄浪空闊
盡吸西江
細斟北斗
萬象爲賓客
扣舷獨笑
不知今夕何夕。

Zhang Xiaoxiang

What a Night!
To the air *Lovely Niannu*

On the grass-green Dongting Lakes,
not a breath of wind,
this close to mid-Autumn:
a jade field, jewelled acres wide,
where my skiff is a little swimming leaf.
Two moons shine,
two silver galaxies gleam,
shimmering brightly above and below.
The heart can easily read such messages,
though their wonder I can't tell you, sir.
I ought to remember long years ago in the South,
when by the gleam of my heart's integrity,
my loyalty shone brighter than the snow.
Though my hair is thin and I'm shivering with cold,
I'll go on drifting on cool waters as broad as the sky above.
The whole of the Western River is pouring out here
for me to ladle it into the stars of the Plough
and buy a drink for all Creation!
Beating time on the gunwale, singing to myself –
what a night! What a night!

Li Bai (701-762)

李白

Cantie ma Lane

自遣

Dram afore uis, A didna see the derknin,
ma claes happit owre wi flouers at fell;
tozie A rise, an follae the mune in the burn,
ilka bird reistit, fowk few an far atween.

對酒不覺暝
落花盈我衣
醉起步溪月
鳥還人亦稀

Cheerful Alone

With drink in front of me, I didn't see it get dark,
and my clothes are covered in fallen flowers;
tipsy I rise and follow the moon in the stream,
every bird gone to roost, and people few and far between.

Book o Sangs
詩經

Anonymous (?11th-7th century BC)

These two poems, adaptations of folksongs from the ancient *Book of Poetry* (*Shi Jing*), were commissioned by Alec Finlay, and appeared in his limited edition artist's book *Carmichael's Book, a Homage to Alexander Carmichael's 'Carmina Gaedelica'*, Artbook and Morning Star: Inverness and Edinburgh (1997).

My brief was to use the original Chinese poems as the basis for my own improvisations, which should closely resemble existing folksongs in Scots or Gaelic. I made some changes to the sense of both, as well as adding a final stanza to the first, and a Gaelic refrain to the second.

The *Book of Songs*, also translated as the *Book of Odes* or the *Classic of Poetry*, is the oldest surviving collection of Chinese poetry. It contains ritual hymns of state, upper-class eulogies, and simple folksongs: its compilation and editing were traditionally ascribed to Confucius. As a revered text throughout Chinese history, it was also highly-regarded in Japan, Korea and Vietnam, making it one of the world's most widely-read books.

Shapit frae *Shaonan No. 20*

gean an rowan fresh an fair
heather white an gowan rare
gin ye lou me
woo me on a lucky day

gean an rowan fresh an fair
heather white an gowan rare
gin ye lou me
woo me, woo me ilka day

gean an rowan fresh an fair
heather white an gowan rare
gin ye lou me
dinna woo, ma lad, juist say

gean an rowan fresh an fair [2]
heather white an gowan rare
gin ye lou me
woo me nou, for A winna stay!

---

[2] This stanza added by BH

召南 摽有梅

摽有梅
其實七兮
求我庶士
迨其吉兮
摽有梅
其實三兮
求我庶士
迨其今兮
摽有梅
頃筐塈之
求我庶士
迨其謂之

Adapted from *Shaonan No. 20*

Wild cherry and mountain ash fresh and fair,
heather white and daisy rare,
if you love me,
woo me on a lucky day.
Wild cherry and mountain ash fresh and fair,
heather white and daisy rare,
if you love me,
woo me, woo me every day.
Wild cherry and mountain ash fresh and fair,
heather white and daisy rare,
if you love me,
don't woo me, my lad, just say.
Wild cherry and mountain ash fresh and fair,
heather white and daisy rare,
if you love me,
woo me now, because I won't stay!

Shapit frae *Odes o Qi No.99*

birslin reid the settin sun
hiri ri mo chridhe
doun she cam sae like the lily
hiri ri mo ghaol
doun she cam intil ma bed
hiri ri mo chridhe
leamin like the settin sun

wae an wae the settin mune
hiri ri mo chridhe
up she gat sae like the lily
hiri ri mo ghaol
frae ma airms awa she gaed
hiri ri mo chridhe
me dwynin like the settin mune

Adapted from Odes of Qi No.99

Scorching red, the setting sun
hiri ri my heart [3]
down she came so like the lily
hiri ri my love
down she came into my bed
hiri ri my heart
glowing like the setting sun.
Woeful, woeful the setting moon
hiri ri my heart
up she got so like the lily
hiri ri my love
from my arms away she went
hiri ri my heart
me fading like the setting moon.

齊風 東方之日

東方之日兮
彼姝者子
在我室兮
在我室兮
履我即兮
東方之月兮
彼姝者子
在我闥兮
在我闥兮
履我發兮

---

[3] Gaelic refrains added by BH

The Nine Sangs
楚辞九歌

屈原

Qu Yuan (329 BC – 299 BC)

Poems 1-4 were originally commissioned by John and Rachel Minford and appeared under the title '*A Wee Pendicle ti 'Songs of the South' bi Dauvit Hawkes*' in their delightful festschrift, *A Birthday Book for Brother Stone: for David Hawkes, at Eighty*, Hong Kong: CUHK Press, 2003; the full set of *Nine Sangs* appeared in *Lallans* 67, Hairst 2005, with a short note on the poems.

I present this sequence in homage to the greatest of Chinese translators, the late David Hawkes (1923-2009), from whom I learned so much.

The text is traditionally attributed to Qu Yuan (343–278 BC), the first named poet in Chinese history, and the progenitor of the annual Dragon Boat Festival, which commemorates his suicide by drowning, as a rebuke to his king. The eleven poems in this section are clearly connected to archaic shamanistic rituals. Perhaps the last two were only sung on particular occasions.

The Nine Sangs

Michtie Monad, Eastren Lord

a seilie day, ay, the hour a luckie ane
mensefu we come, see, ti ser the Lord Abune
claymores in haun, ay, aa jade-heftit
gemstanes jinglin, see, wi sardane an wi beriall
wi jowelt rugs, ay, an wechts o jade
sae beir awa, see, the flouerie offrands
mappiemou mait, ay, an mats o the mascorn
pour the cannel yill, see, the pepperie brose
lift the tipper, ay, an touk the bodhran
hoolie the urlar, see, an slaw the sang
clarsach an chanter, ay, a sonsie skirl
hie-heidit the Cailleach, see, brankit sae brawlie
wi ferlie oams, ay, the haas are fou
the Five Souns monieplied, see, mellit thegither
the Lord taks pleasance o't, ay, crouse-like an cantie

東皇太一

吉日兮辰良
穆將愉兮上皇
撫長劍兮玉珥
璆鏘鳴兮琳瑯
瑤席兮玉瑱
盍將把兮瓊芳
蕙肴蒸兮蘭藉
奠桂酒兮椒漿
揚枹兮拊鼓
疏緩節兮安歌
陳竽瑟兮浩倡
靈偃蹇兮姣服
芳菲菲兮滿堂
五音兮繁會
君欣欣兮樂康

Mighty Monad, Lord of the East

A blessed day, the hour a lucky one,
respectfully we come to serve the Lord Above,
in hand swords all jade-hefted,
gemstones jinging with cornelian and beryl,
with jewelled rugs and weights of jade.
So bear away the flowery offerings,
snapdragon meats and mats of silverweed;
pour the cinnamon ale, the peppery broth.
Lift the drumstick and strike the frame drum;
the theme is adagio, slow is the song,
harp and shawm, a full-bodied sound.
Proud is the Old Woman, in such fine array.
With faerie airs the halls are full,
the Five Musical notes multiplied and mixed together:
the Lord takes pleasure in it, cheerful and merry.

Lord Inben the Clouds

doukit wi spykarie, ay, locks wuishen sweet
claes o monie colours, see, braw wi the gingie-flouer
souple bends the Cailleach, ay, the Speirit's upon her
leamin in the lowe o't, see, mair yit ti come
sirs, he's ti rest, ay, i the Hous o Lang Life
like the sun and the mune, see, burnin sae bricht
dragon yokit, ay, wi mantill imperiall
nou the Speirit's on the stravaig, see, reingin aa roun
the Cailleach's fair a ferlie, ay, nou come doun
on a suddentie the Speirit flees, see, inben the clouds
he owreleuks the Nor-East, ay, an faur ayont it
the Fower Seas he traivels, see, an whae wad stent him?
think lang on the Lord, ay, an mak great mane
be byornar hertsair, see, doilt wi dule.

雲中君

浴蘭湯兮沐芳
華采衣兮若英
靈連蜷兮既留
爛昭昭兮未央
騫將憺兮壽宮
與日月兮齊光
龍駕兮帝服
聊翱游兮周章
靈皇皇兮既降
猋遠舉兮雲中
覽冀洲兮有余
橫四海兮焉窮
思夫君兮太息
極勞心兮忡忡

Lord Within the Clouds

Drenched in spikenard, hair washed and sweet,
clothes of many colours, handsome with ginger-flower,
supple the Old Woman bends, the Spirit upon her,
glowing in the gleam of it, with more still to come.
Sirs, he will rest in the House of Long Life:
like the sun and moon, he's burning so bright,
with his dragon harnessed, and his imperial mantle.
Now the Spirit is on the move, ranging all around.
The Old Woman's a wonder, now come down;
suddenly the Spirit flies within the clouds;
he looks out over the North-East and far beyond:
he travels the Four Seas, and who would limit him?
Think long on the Lord and make a loud moan,
be extraordinarily sore at heart, maddened with grief.

Leddy o the Xiang Watter

the Leddy disna muve, ay, she's switherin
eh, whae is't waitin, see, awa on the annay?
weill-faured an lousome, ay, buskit sae brawlie
smoothlie A skiff, see, in cannel-wuid coble
Yuan an Xiang Watters, ay, smaa be yir waves
Lang Watter o Yangzi, see, saft may ye rin
A weary for the Leddy, ay, she still hesna come
wheeplin on her pipe, see, wha does she think on?
fleein dragon yokit, ay, norlin A gang
roun-about ma road, see, ti the Lochs o Dongting
bindwood palins, ay, bund wi curl-doddie
graith o the seggans, see, pensell o the soucie
leukin owre ti Chenyang, ay, on the ither shore
owre the Muckle Watter, see, lat aefauldness be kent
lat aefauldness be kent, ay, tho it hesna happent yit
sweir is ma sister, see, makin mane for me
A think lang on the Leddy, ay, tho laich be ma place
airs o cannel-wuid, see, helmstock o the mascorn
kirnin at the ice, ay, freithin't inti snaa
pou the bindwuid, see, out the watter
pouk the lillie, ay, doun frae the treetap
hairts no ane, see, a warsle for the match-wyfe
hairt-likin no deep, ay, licht'll be the twynin
river rack, see, pirlin an papplin
fleein dragon, ay, flichterin an flaffin
forgaitherin no leal-hairtit, see, lang'll be the canker o't
ye keepitna the tryst, ay, said ye'd nae by-time
i the dawin A skelp, see, owre watterside mosses
i the gloamin A rest, ay, on the Norlan Annay
birds reist, see, on ma riggin-heid

湘君

君不行兮夷犹
蹇誰留兮中洲
美要眇兮宜修
沛吾乘兮桂舟
令沅湘兮無波
使江水兮安流
望夫君兮未来
吹参差兮谁思
駕飛龍兮北征
邅吾道兮洞庭
薜荔柏兮蕙綢
荪桡兮蘭旌
望涔阳兮极浦
橫大江兮扬靈
扬靈兮未極
女嬋媛兮為余太息
橫流涕兮潺湲
隱思君兮陫側
桂櫂兮兰枻
斲冰兮積雪
采薜荔兮水中
搴芙蓉兮木末
心不同兮媒勞
恩不甚兮輕絕
石瀨兮淺淺
飛龍兮翩翩
交不忠兮怨長
期不信兮告余以不閑
朝騁騖兮江皋
夕弭節兮北渚

Lady of the River Xiang

The Lady doesn't move, she's hesitating:
oh, who is it waiting over on the river island?
Good-looking and loveable, so beautifully arrayed,
smoothly I skim, in a cinnamon-wood boat.
Yuan and Xiang Rivers, small be your waves;
long River Yangzi, soft may you run.
I long for the Lady, but still she hasn't come.
Whistling on her pipe, who is she thinking about?
Flying dragon harnessed, northwards I go,
round-about is my road, to the Lakes of Dongting.
Woodbine fences bound with scabious,
my tackle of wild iris and my pennant of orchids,
looking over to Chenyang on the other shore,
over the Great River, let my sincerity be known;
let my sincerity be known, though that hasn't happened yet.
Idle is my sister, making her moan for me.
I think long on the Lady, though low be my place.
Oars of cinnamon wood, tiller of silverweed,
churning the ice, frothing it into snow;
pull the bindweed out from the water,
pluck the lily down from the treetop.
Hearts not united, a struggle for the match-maker;
heart's liking not deep, light will be the parting.
River rapids whirling and rippling,
a flying dragon, fluttering and flapping.
If the meeting isn't sincere, then long will be the grudge.
You didn't keep the tryst, said you'd no time.
In the dawn I scamper over riverside marshes,
at twilight I rest on the Northern River-Island.
Birds roost on my rooftree, water runs all round my house:

watter rins, ay, aa roun ma hous
A'll birl ma ring o jade, see, intil the Lang Watter
A'll fling ma enseignies, ay, in the Douce Burn
on Perfumit Annay, see, gaitherin the gingie-flouer
A'll haun it aa doun, ay, ti you yins at comes efter
this tid canna weill, see, be twice taen
A'm gaun raikin a whylie, ay, ti play on in pleasure

鳥次兮屋上
水周兮堂下
捐余玦兮江中
遗余佩兮醴浦
采芳洲兮杜若
将以遗兮下女
時不可兮再得
聊逍遥兮容与

I'll toss my ring of jade into the Great River,
I'll fling my insignia in the Sweet Stream,
on Perfumed River-Island gathering ginger-flowers,
I'll hand it all down to you who come after.
This chance won't easily be taken twice:
I'm off wandering for a while, to play on at my pleasure.

Guidwyfe o the Xiang Watter

dochter o a god, ay, on the norlan annay
hyne-awa leukin, see, maks uis hairt-sair
wind o hairst, ay, souchin, souchin
faain leafs, see, on Dongting's waves
on white seggans steppin, ay, A leuk outbye
trystit wi her, see, ahint hingins at een
hou's the birds forgaitherin, ay, awa i the rashes?
hou's the fishin nets, see, up i the treetaps?
angelica on Yuan Watter, ay, mascorn on the Li
for thinkin lang on Ma Leddy, see, A daurna tell
drowie, drumlie, ay, leukin farawa
watchin the rinnin, see, o watter onendin
hou's hert an hind, ay, inben the close?
hou's the burn dragons, see, up on the haughs?
i the dawin A ride, see, owre watterside mosses
i the gloamin A rest, ay, on the Westlin Carse
A hear ma luve, see, she's cryin on me
hurlin in ma cairtie, ay, we'll wheech awa thegither
we'll bigg a hous, see, in ablow the watter
theik the riggin, see, wi leafs o the lillie
waas o the seggan, ay, an purpie-wulk chaumers
tak perfumit peppers, see, ti mak the haas
cabers o the cannel, ay, an spykarie bauks
lintels o magnolia, see, bouer o angelica
wuiven bindwuid, ay, ti mak the hingins
owretrees o riven mappie-mou, see, for the easins
white jade, ay, for the haa
skail stane-gress, see, for its sweet smell
theikit wi angelica, ay, chaumer o the lotus
weill-wappit, see, wi cammavine

湘夫人 / Goodwife of the River Xiang

帝子降兮北渚
目眇眇兮愁予
裊裊兮秋風
洞庭波兮木葉下
登白蘋兮騁望
與佳期兮夕張
鳥何萃兮蘋中
罾何為兮木上
沅有茝兮醴有蘭
思公子兮未敢言
荒忽兮遠望
觀流水兮潺湲
麋何食兮庭中
蛟何為兮水裔
朝馳余馬兮江皋
夕濟兮西澨
聞佳人兮召余
將騰駕兮偕逝
筑室兮水中
葺之兮荷蓋
蓀壁兮紫壇
播芳椒兮成堂
桂棟兮蘭橑
辛夷楣兮藥房
罔薜荔兮為帷
擗蕙櫋兮既張
白玉兮為鎮
疏石蘭兮為芳
芷葺兮荷屋
繚之兮杜衡

Daughter of a god on the northern river-island,
looking far away makes me heart-sore;
autumn wind soughing, soughing,
fallen leaves on Dongting waves;
on white iris stepping I look into the distance,
having arranged to meet her behind the hangings at evening.
Why are the birds gathering, away in the rushes?
Why are the fish nets up in the treetops?
Angelica on the Yuan River, silverweed on the Li:
yearning for My Lady, I daren't tell;
looking far away into the vague and indistinct distance,
watching the running of water unending.
Why are hart and hind inside the farmyard?
Why are the stream dragons up on the banks?
In the dawn I ride over riverside marshes,
in the twilight I rest on the Western Flats.
I hear my love, she's calling to me:
riding in my carriage, we'll whizz away together;
we'll build a house in below the water,
thatch the roof with leaves of the lily,
walls of iris, and whelk-purple chambers.
Take perfumed peppers to make the halls,
rafters of cinnamon and spikenard beams,
lintels of magnolia, bower of angelica;
woven bindweed to make the hangings,
joists of split snapdragon for the eaves,
white jade for the hall.
Scatter stone-grass for its sweet smell;
thatch of angelica, bedchamber of lotus,
well-bound with chamomile:

hunners o flouers, ay, fillin the haa
sweet oams skailin, see, in througang an yett
thrang on Mount Mislippen, ay, meetin thegither
comin o the speirits, see, monie as the clouds
A'll birl ma ring o jade, see, intil the Muckle Watter
A'll fling ma cuttie serk, ay, in the Douce Burn
On Peacefu Haughs, see, A'll pouk the gingie-flouer
an sen it, ay, ti Her Hyneawa
time canna weill, see, be taen mair as yince
A'll raik on a whylie, ay, ti play on in pleisure

合百草兮實庭
建芳馨兮廡門
九嶷繽兮并迎
靈之來兮如雲
捐余袂兮江中
遺余褋兮醴浦
搴汀洲兮杜若
將以遺兮遠者
時不可兮驟得
聊逍遙兮容與

hundreds of flowers filling the hall,
sweet aromas drifting in corridor and doorway.
Thronging on Mount Misdoubt, meeting together,
the coming of the spirits, many as the clouds.
I'll toss my ring of jade into the Great River;
I'll fling my tunic in the Sweet Stream.
On Peaceful Holms I'll pluck the ginger-flower,
and send it to Her Faraway.
A season cannot well be taken more than once:
I'll wander on for a while, to play on at pleasure.

Greater Lord o Fate

apen braid, ay, the yetts o the lift
a ferlie am A, see, i the mirk o the cairrie
A gar whidderin wunds, ay, gang on afore uis
mak the onding, see, lay aa the stour
brallin and tovin, ay, doun comes the Lord nou
A follaed ye, see, ayont Tuimberry Hill
thrangin fowk, ay, o aa the Nine Lands
yir lifes and yir daiths, see, is aa doun ti me
he's fleein hie abune, ay, tovin slaw
ridin Pure Braith, see, caain Yin an Yang
A'll gaun wi ye lord, ay, as gleg as yirsel
leadin ye, see, doun the Nine Delfs
lang lang, ay, is ma warlock-kirtle
glorious, see, ma gemstane girdle
aa o the Yin, ay, an aa o the Yang
fowk disna ken, see, the things A can dae
pouk the Halie Hemp, ay, wi jowelt flouers vieve an white
an gift them, see, ti Him at's hyneawa
bit an bi bit, ay, it's auld A've gotten
niver nae nearer, see, aye faurer awa
ridin the draigon cairt, ay, wi dunnerin wheels
ramstam ridin, see, He's awa ti the lift
poukin the cannel beuchs, ay, A'm lang an lang stellit
wearyin for Him, see, sair's ma hairt
sair's ma hairt, ay, but whit can A dae?
o gin naethin wad cheinge, see, but bide like the nou
for fowk's lifes, ay, is weirdit ilkane
meetins an pairtins, see, wha'll can guide them?

大司命

廣開兮天門
紛吾乘兮玄雲
令飄風兮先驅
使凍雨兮灑塵
君回翔兮以下
逾空桑兮從女
紛總總兮九州
何壽夭兮在予
高飛兮安翔
乘清氣兮御陰陽
吾與君兮齊速
導帝之兮九坑
靈衣兮被被
玉佩兮陸離
一陰兮一陽
眾莫知兮余所為
折疏麻兮瑤華
將以遺兮離居
老冉冉兮既極
不寖近兮愈疏
乘龍兮轔轔
高馳兮沖天
結桂枝兮延佇
羌愈思兮愁人
愁人兮奈何
願若今兮無虧
固人命兮有當
孰離合兮何為

Greater Lord of Fate

Open wide the gates of the sky:
a wonder am I in the dark of the clouds.
I make the whirling winds go on before me,
make the storm lay all the dust.
Soaring and rising in the air,
down comes the Lord now.
I followed you beyond Toomberry Hill.
Thronging folk of all the Nine Lands,
your lives and your deaths are all down to me.
He's flying high above, slowly wheeling,
riding Pure Breath, driving Yin and Yang.
I'll go with you, lord, as quick as yourself,
leading you down the Nine Deeps.
Long, long is my warlock-coat,
glorious, my gemstone girdle;
all of the Yin, and all of the Yang:
folk don't know the things I can do.
Pluck the Holy Hemp with jeweled flowers bright and pale,
and give them to Him that's faraway.
Bit by bit, it's old I've grown:
never any nearer, but always farther away.
Riding the dragon carriage with thundering wheels,
riding headlong, He's gone to the sky.
Plucking the cinnamon boughs, I've long been stuck,
longing for Him, sore is my heart.
Sore is my heart, but what can I do?
O that nothing would change, but stay like it is now,
for folk's lives are fated every one:
meetings and partings, who can control them?

Lesser Lord o Fate

mascorn o the hairst, see, an deer's gerss tae
spreid aa about, ay, there ablow the haa
leaf o the green, see, an flourish o the white
perfumit pirls, ay, wimplin aa about uis
the Guidman hissel, see, hes bairnies sae braw
sae hou is the seggans, ay, hairtsair wi dule?
mascorn o the hairst, see, wi emerant hue
leaf o the green, ay, shank o the white
fu is the hous, see, o beauties sae braw
but swith his een, ay, ti me alane cam
wi nae word he cam in, see, an wi nane he gaed out
ridin the whidderin wunds, ay, drowie pensells flaffin
sairest o sorras, see, them on life at maun sinder
brawest of blitheness, ay, trystit wi a new frein
wi lillie-leaf coatie, see, an mappie-mou sash
swith cam he in, ay, an swipper he gaed
the nicht he'll stop, see, i the Hous o the Hie Ane
at the cairrie's en, ay, wha're ye waitin on?
stravaigin awa wi ye, see, owre the Nine Watters
wi ramballiach reishle, ay, wunds blatter the waves
A'll wesh ma hair wi ye, see, i the Stank o the Lift
ye'll dicht yir hair, ay, on the Skerrs o the Sun
A grein for the Braw Ane, see, at still hesna come
radge i the wund, ay, rairin out ma sang
wi paycock baudkin, see, and halcyon pensell
he sclims the Ninefauld Lift, ay, an cleiks the Besom Staur
branglin his muckle claymore, see, beildin young an auld
ma Sweet Ane alane worthie, ay, ti hae dominion owre the fowk

少司命　　　　　　　　　　　　　*Lesser Lord of Fate*

秋蘭兮麇蕪　　　　　　Silver weed of autumn, and deer-grass too,
羅生兮堂下　　　　　　　spread all about, there below the hall;
綠葉兮素華　　　　　　　　leaf of green and blossoms of white,
芳菲菲兮襲予　　　　　perfumed breezes meandering around me.
夫人兮自有美子　　　　The Goodman himself has children so lovely.
蓀何以兮愁苦　　　　　So why is the iris heart-sore with grief?
秋蘭兮青青　　　　　　Silverweed of autumn, with emerald hue;
綠葉兮紫莖　　　　　　　leaf of green, stem of white:
滿堂兮美人　　　　　　　full is the house, with beauties so fine.
忽獨與余兮目成　　　　Suddenly his eyes to me alone came;
入不言兮出不辭　　　with no word he came in, and with none he went out,
乘回風兮載雲旗　　　riding the whirling winds, misty pennants flapping.
悲莫愁兮生別離　　　Sorest of sorrows, those that must in this life sunder;
樂莫樂兮新相知　　　　bravest of blitheness, meeting a new friend.
荷衣兮蕙帶　　　　　　　With lily-leaf coat, and snapdragon sash,
儵而來兮忽而逝　　　　suddenly came he in, and swiftly he went:
夕宿兮帝郊　　　　　　tonight he'll stay in the House of the High One.
君誰須兮雲之際　　　At the edge of the overcast sky, who are you waiting for?
與女沐兮咸池　　　　　Gallivanting away with you over the Nine Rivers,
晞女髮兮陽之阿　　　　with stormy clatter winds batter the waves.
望美人兮未來　　　　　I'll wash my hair with you in the Pool of the Sky;
臨風怳兮好歌　　　　　you'll dry your hair on the Crags of the Sun:
孔蓋兮翠旌　　　　　　I yearn for the Lovely One who still hasn't come,
登九天兮撫彗星　　　　crazy in the wind, roaring out my song.
竦長劍兮擁幼艾　　　　With peacock canopy and kingfisher pennant,
蓀獨宜兮為民正　　he climbs the Nine-fold Sky and catches the Broomstick Star.
　　　　　　　Brandishing his huge claymore, protector of young and old,
　　　　my Sweet one, alone worthy to have dominion over the people.

Lord o the East

blinterin A rise, see, eastawa
brichten ma door-stane, ay, the Dawin Tree
A clap ma naigie, see, an gang hoolie forrit
the gloamin greys, ay, an day grows bricht
caain ma draigon cairtie, see, the thunner-rider
drowie pensells flaffin, ay, flochterin an flingin
the ae lang souch, see, an A maun rise
switherin in ma hairt, ay, wearyin an leukin on
och the music an the dancin, see, they'd beglamour a bodie
them at's leukin, ay, disremember ti gang hame
kittle up the tiompan, see, an touk the drums thegither
ding the bells, see, an gar the gantrees dirl
soun the feadogs, ay, an blaw the pipes
deek ye the Cailleachs, see, weill-faurd an wycelike
sweilin an birlin, ay, fliein hie abune
rowin out the sang, see, linkin thegither
cannie the canntaireachd, ay, weill-cordit the lilt
the Speirit's come doun, see, smoorit's the sun
cled wi the cairrie, ay, watergaw-kiltit
A vizzy ma lang arra, see, an shuit the Wowf o the Lift
raxin out the Bou Staur, ay, sae comes ma doungang
cleikin the Pleuch, see, to pour ma cannel yill
grippin ma reins, ay, breingin dounby
ti the howe o the derk, see, eastawa farin

東君

暾將出兮東方
吾檻兮扶桑
撫余馬兮安驅
夜皎皎兮既明
駕龍輈兮乘雷
載雲旗兮委蛇
長太息兮將上
心低徊兮顧懷
羌聲色兮娛人
觀者憺兮忘歸
緪瑟兮交鼓
簫鐘兮瑤簴
鳴篪兮吹竽
思靈保兮賢姱
翾飛兮翠曾
展詩兮會舞
應律兮合節
靈之來兮敝日
青雲衣兮白霓裳
舉長矢兮射天狼
操余弧兮反淪降
援北斗兮酌桂漿
撰余轡兮高馳翔
杳冥冥兮以東行

Lord of the East

Blazing I rise east away,
and brighten my door-stone, the Dawn Tree;
I pat my horse and go slowly forward,
the twilight turns grey, and day grows bright.
Driving my dragon carriage, the thunder-rider,
misty pennants flapping, fluttering and dancing.
One long sigh, and I must rise,
uncertain in my heart, longing and looking –
Oh, the music and the dancing, they'd bewitch anyone:
those who are watching forget to go home.
Strike up the dulcimer, and beat the drums all together;
ring the bells, and make the rafters ring.
Sound the whistles, and blow the pipes:
See the Old Women, good-looking and wise,
swirling and spinning, flying high above,
singing out the song, dancing together.
Pleasant the chanting, harmonious the rhythm.
The Spirit has come down, smothered is the sun,
clad in the clouds, rainbow-skirted.
I sight my long arrow and shoot the Wolf of Heaven,
reaching past the Bow Star, and so comes my descent.
Catching hold of the big Dipper to pour my cinnamon ale,
gripping the reins, and plunging down
to the depths of the darkness, travelling eastward.

Yerl o the Watters

stravaigin wi ye, see, owre the Nine Watters
wi ramballiach reishle, ay, winds blatter the waves
hurlin in ma watter-cairtie, see, wi ruif o the lillies
caain twa kelpies but, ay, an twa dragons ben
speilin the Hallow Hill, see, leukin owre ilka airt
hairt lowp-lowpin, ay, dirlin wi joy
sun's at the gloamin, see, A'm gled an sweir ti gang hame
och yon ferawa shore, ay, heizes up ma hairt
fish-scale courts, see, an dragon haas
yetts o the purpie wulk, ay, an chaumers o the crammasie
whit's the Speirit daein, see, doun ablow the watter?
striddlin the white turtle, ay, huntin sprecklt fish
stravaigin wi ye, see, owre the annays
thrang wi the snaabree, ay, the Maister comes doun
ye chap hauns, see, eastawa gangin
convoyin ma beauty, ay, ti the suddron shore
sweelin swaws, see, forgaither wi me
the tane efter the tither, ay, ma menyie o fish

河伯

與女游兮九河
沖風起兮水揚波
乘水車兮荷蓋
駕兩龍兮驂螭
登昆侖兮四望
心飛揚兮浩蕩
日將暮兮悵忘歸
惟極浦兮寤懷
魚鱗屋兮龍堂
紫貝闕兮珠宮
靈何惟兮水中
乘白黿兮逐文魚
與女游兮河之渚
流澌紛兮將來下
子交手兮東行
送美人兮南浦
波滔滔兮來迎
魚鱗鱗兮媵予

Earl of the Rivers

Wandering with you over the Nine Rivers,
with stormy clatter winds batter the waves,
riding in my water-carriage, with its roof of lilies,
driving two dragons on the inside, and two kelpies on the outside.
Climbing Mount Kunlun, looking out in every direction,
heart leaping, tingling with joy:
the sun's at the gloaming, I'm glad and unwilling to go home –
oh, that faraway shore lifts up my heart.
Fish-scale courts and dragon halls,
gates of purple whelk, and chambers of crimson.
What's the Spirit doing, down below the water?
Straddling the white turtle, hunting speckled fish,
wandering with you over the river-islands.
Full of snow-melt, the Master comes down;
you clap hands, going eastward,
conveying my beauty to the southern shores.
Swirling waves come to meet me,
one after the other, my following of fishes.

Guidwyfe o the Ben

it's like the'r a bodie, see, i the lirk o the ben
happit wi the bindwuid, ay, beltit wi the leddy-fern
een hauflins steikit, see, an a bonnie smile
ye're browdent on me, ay, gleg ti beglamour me
caain the reid panthers, see, follain the lyart tods
magnolia cairtie, ay, cannel-weavit pensel
happit wi the spykarie, see, beltit wi the lilly-flouer
poukin rare perfumes, ay, ti gie ti her jo
A byde i the derk shaws, see, at niver sees the cairrie
sair an unchancie the road, ay, an me come ahint-haun
staunin ma lane, see, at the heid o the hill
rowin cluds, ay, aa ablow me
i the howe o the derk, see, mirk in braid day
easslin wunds risin, ay, douncome o ferlie rain
the Carline dawdles blythelike, see, an disremembers ti gang hame
the year's that worn doun, ay, whaur's ma flouers nou?
A'll pouk the treeple orchids, see, in atween the bens
whaur clintie's the stanes, ay, mang rammels o the brier
A grein for Himsel, see, an disremember ti gang hame
ye think lang on me, see, but haena onie by-time
the bodie mang the bens, ay, i the scug o pine an cypress
ye think lang on me, see, but ye're switherin yet
thunner's dirl-dirlin, see, an mirksome's the rain
yatterin o puggies, ay, apes yowlin under nicht
gurlie an gowstie's the wund, see, hushlin mang the shaws
A think lang on Hersel, ay, an tuim's ma dule an wae

山鬼

若有人兮山之阿
被薛荔兮帶女蘿
既含睇兮又宜笑
子慕予兮善窈窕
乘赤豹兮从文狸
辛夷車兮結桂旗
被石蘭兮帶杜衡
折芬馨兮遺所思
余處幽篁兮終不見天
路險難兮獨后來
表獨立兮山之上
雲容容兮而在下
杳冥冥兮羌晝晦
東風飄兮神靈雨
留靈修兮憺忘歸
歲既晏兮孰華予
采三秀兮于山間
石磊磊兮葛蔓蔓
怨公子兮悵忘歸
君思我兮不得閑
山中人兮芳杜若
飲石泉兮蔭松柏
君思我兮然疑作
雷填填兮雨冥冥
猿啾啾兮狖夜鳴
風颯颯兮木蕭蕭
思公子兮徒離憂

Goodwife of the Mountain

It seems there's someone, in a fold of the hill,
dressed in bindweed, belted with lichen,
eyes half shut, and a lovely smile.
You adore me, you're keen to enchant me,
leading red panthers, following speckled foxes;
magnolia carriage, cinnamon-woven pennant;
dressed in spikenard, belted with the lily-flower,
picking rare perfumes, to give to her love.
I live in dark woods, that never see the sky.
Hard and dangerous the road, and I have come late.
Standing alone at the top of the hill, rolling clouds all below me;
in the hollow of the darkness, obscure in broad daylight,
eastern winds rising, falling of divine rain.
The Crone dawdles happily, and forgets to go home.
The year is so worn out, and where are my flowers now?
I'll pluck the triple orchids, in between the mountains,
rocky among brushwood and briar.
I yearn for Himself and forget to go home.
You think long on me, but have no spare time.
Someone's among the hills, in the shade of cypress and pine.
You think long on me, but you're still hesitating;
thunder's rumbling, and it's dark in the rain:
chattering of monkeys, apes howling by night;
blustery and gusty is the wind, whistling through the woods.
I think long on Herself, and empty is my grief and woe.

Flouers o the Forest

grippin swuirds frae the south, ay, an jacks o fine leather
wheel-nave ti wheel-nave, see, the gullie-men yoke thegither
pensells smoor the sun, ay, faes like fleein clouds forgaither
arras faa in ilka airt, see, sodgers wraslin forrit
they brash throu the array, ay, strampin on the lines
the land-horse is deid, see, an the fore ane's dung doun
baith wheels lairit in glaur, ay, an the fowersome aa fanklt
grip the jade tipper, see, an touk the roarin drum
the day's weirin doun, ay, an the great gods are beilin
they're slauchtert aa an haill, see, forhooiet on the field
they gaed out an niver cam in, ay, gaed an niver wan hame
they hap aa the haughs, see, here an hyne owre yonder
braid swuirds at their sides, ay, they grippit norlan bous
tho heids frae bouks wis sindert, see, aa their hairts wir leal
stalwart ti the last, ay, nane can them miscaa
tho cauld be their corps, see, on life are their speirits
sodgers, yir sowls, ay, are heroes ayont the graff

國殤

操吳戈兮被犀甲
車錯轂兮短兵接
旌蔽日兮敵若雲
矢交墜兮士爭先
凌余陣兮躐余行
左驂殪兮右刃傷
霾兩輪兮縶四馬
援玉枹兮擊鳴鼓
天時墜兮威靈怒
嚴殺盡兮棄原野
出不入兮往不反
平原忽兮路超遠
帶長劍兮挾秦弓
首身離兮心不懲
誠既勇兮又以武
終剛強兮不可凌
身既死兮神以靈
魂魄亦兮為鬼雄

Flowers of the Forest [4]

Gripping swords from the south, in jerkins of fine leather,
wheel-hub to wheel-hub, the short-sword men come to grips;
pennants smother the sun, foes like flying clouds forgather.
Arrows fall in every direction, soldiers wrestling forward;
they rush through the array, trampling on the lines.
The left-hand horse is dead, and the right-hand one's knocked down,
both wheels stuck in mud, and the four-in-hand tangled up.
Grip the jade drumstick, and beat the roaring drum,
the day's wearing down, and the great gods are angry.
Slaughtered every one, forsaken on the field,
they went out and never came in, went and never came home:
they cover all the plain, here and far over yonder.
Broad swords at their sides, they grasped northern bows;
though heads from bodies were sundered, all their hearts were true;
stalwart to the last, none can speak ill of them:
though cold be their corpses, alive are their spirits.
Soldiers, your souls are heroes beyond the grave.

---

[4] The title here could be literally rendered by "dying too young for the sake of the nation". In the interests of concision, I have borrowed the title of the old Border lament to translate the connotative sense of the original.

The Sainin o Sowls

dune is the sainin, see, wi monie's the drum
frae haun ti haun gae the flouers, ay, ti dancers ane an bi ane
maidens aa liltin, see, houlie an slaw
mascorns i the waretime, ay, an chrysanths i the hairst
sae maun it be, see, for aye an for aye

sae maun it be, see, for aye an for aye

禮魂

成禮兮會鼓，
傳芭兮代舞；
姱女倡兮容與；
春蘭兮秋菊，
長無絕兮終古。

The Hallowing of Souls

Done is the hallowing, with many a drum;
from hand to hand go the flowers, to dancers one by one,
maidens all singing softly and slow.
Silverweed in the spring, and chrysanthemums in the autumn –
so must it be, for ever and ever.

So must it be, for ever and ever.[5]

---

[5] Repetition added by BH

The Sage o Poetry
詩聖

Du Fu (712-770)
杜甫

Du Fu (712-770) is one of the greatest of all Chinese poets, and though he was high-born, a distant, poor relative of the Imperial family, his career was not a glorious one, and he was more than once seconded to junior posts in remote regions, or stranded by rebellions and border wars. He knew the meaning of sorrow and grief – one of his children died of hunger during a prolonged absence – but transmuted this personal pain into hauntingly beautiful verse of great grandeur and complexity, poetry which is wittily innovative, and almost impudently virtuosic. Though written with impressive technical bravura, many of his poems are like short, heart-rendingly sad jokes.

These poems are written in the New Style Regulated Verse stanza, a form of considerable difficulty which demands simultaneous verbal, symbolic and syntactic parallelism within a tight rhyme scheme, and is built around a strict metric pattern which uses, not stress or length, but tones – the built-in pitch contours of the Chinese syllable – as its foundation.

'Spring Sun on the Watterside Clachan' was awarded a Commendation in the *Times* Stephen Spender Poetry Translation Prize, 2012.

'Hairst-Time Quicknin' appeared in *Renditions* 74, Autumn 2010, as part of *Du Fu: A Poem and a Provocation.*

Frae Hie Abune

a grumlie gowl, the lift hie abune
puggies greit an mane
caller annays, white sauns
birds flee hame ti reist
nae en o failin trees, leafs
faan i the reishlin wund
ne'er still, the Muckle Watter
rowin an pirlin doun
a thousan mile o hert-sair hairsts –
an here's me, fremt for ay
a lang life o seikness tae –
sclimmin the touer ma lane
cark an care an wersh wersh rue
an cranreuch at ma haffets
a pugglt auld gangrel – an juist gied
up the bluidie booze

登高

風急天高猿嘯哀
渚清沙白鳥飛回
無邊落木蕭蕭下
不盡長江袞袞來
萬里悲秋常作客
百年多病獨登臺
艱難苦恨繁霜鬢
潦倒新停濁酒杯

From High Above

A grumbling gale, sky high above,
    apes howl and moan.
Fresh river-islands, white sands,
    birds fly home to roost.
No end of failing trees,
    leaves failing in the rustling wind.
Never still, the Great River,
    rolling and rippling down.
A thousand miles of heart-sore harvests –
    and here's me, always a stranger:
a long life of sickness too – climbing the tower alone;
    worry and care and bitter regrets,
    and hoar-frost at my temples.
A worn-out old vagrant –
    and just given up the bloody booze!

Quatrains   絕句

i

our land's gey bonnie i the settin sun
gress and flouers perfumin the waretime wund
swallas flee abune the slaistery slatch
doverin deuks beik on the warm saun

一
遲日江山麗
春風花草香
泥融飛燕子
沙暖睡鴛鴦

ii

the watter's emerant, the birds whiter yit
the hills is green, their flourish skyrie-gettin
here's anither waretime winnin awa –
an whan'll come ma ain hame-gaun?

二
江碧鳥逾白
山青花欲燃
今春看又過
何日是歸年

Quatrains

i

Our land is lovely in the setting sun,
grass and flowers perfuming the springtime breeze;
swallows fly above the wet mud,
dozing ducks bask on the warm sand.

ii

The river's emerald, the birds whiter yet,
the hills are green, their foliage getting brighter:
here's another springtime departing –
and when will come my own home-going?

對雪

戰哭多新鬼
愁吟獨老翁
亂雲低薄暮
急雪舞回風
瓢棄樽無綠
爐存火似紅
數州消息斷
愁坐正書空

Forenent the Snaa

war, an greitin, an monie new ghaists
chantin doul an wae, an auld bodach his lane
the tapsalteerie cairrie's gaun doun ti dayset
flauchts o snaa dancin i the whidderin wund
the caup's cuisten awa, an the coggie's tuim
but the stove's there yit, an fair like reid
sindert frae the stewartries, nae news at aa
here's me, sittin waefu, scrievin i the air

Facing the Snow

War, and weeping, and many new ghosts:
chanting grief and woe, an old man on his own.
The tumbling clouds are going down to sunset,
flights of snow dancing in the whirling wind,
the ladle is cast away and the punchbowl is empty,
but the stove's still there, and seems to be red.
Cut off from the provinces, no news at all,
and here I am, sitting woefully writing in the air.

The Watterside Clachan

wi the ae jouk the caller watter
oxters the clachan as it rins
this watterside clachan aa summer
lithe an lown it lies
the swallas is aye joukin in an out
amang the riggin-trees
an seamaas coorie in aa crouse
thegither on the watter
the cailleach scrieves hersel a paper
ti mak a dambrod o't
the younkers chap awa at preens
ti mak their fishin heuks
gin A hed a guid auld frein
ti help wi meal an siller
a simple hameart sowl like me –
whit ither wad A seek for?

江 村

清江一曲抱村流
長夏江村事事幽
自去自來梁上燕
相親相近水中鷗
老妻畫紙為棋局
稚子敲針作釣鉤
但有故人供祿米
微軀此外更何求

The Riverside Hamlet

Within a single bend the clear river
enfolds the hamlet as it flows;
this riverside hamlet lies quiet and peaceful
all summer long.
The swallows are always ducking
in an out among the roof-beams,
and seagulls cuddling cosily
together on the river.
My old wife scribes herself a paper
to make a draughtboard;
the young ones hammer away at pins
to make their fish-hooks.
Supposing I had a good old friend
to help with food and money –
a simple homebody like me –
what else would I seek for?

The Walcome
Fair pleased at ma kizzen
H.E. Shirra Cui cryin in…

besouth an benorth ma but an ben
naethin but waretime fluidin
naethin ti see bar seamaas in flochts
comin day an daily
ma flouerie bauks hes niver yit
been soupit for a veisitor
ma wicker yett for the firsten time
'll open for ye the day, sir
fancy breid? the mercat's fer
there'll be naethin ti gust yir gab, sir
a gless, ye say? it's a tuim wee hous
forbye oor fernyear's brewin
but gin ye're willin to cowp a gless
wi the auld bodach at's ma neibour
A'll cry him in outowre the dyke
an we'll tak a rowth o drams thegither

客 至
喜崔明府相過

舍南舍北皆春水
但見群鷗日日來
花徑不曾緣客掃
蓬門今始為君開
盤飧市遠無兼味
樽酒家貧只舊醅
肯與鄰翁相對飲
隔籬呼取盡余杯

The Welcome
Really pleased at my cousin
H.E. Sheriff Cui calling on me…

South and north of my little cottage,
nothing but spring floods,
nothing to see but seagulls in flocks
daily flying over;
my flower-grown paths have never yet
been swept for a visitor,
my wicker gate for the first time
will open for you today, sir.
Fancy bread? the market's faraway:
there'll be nothing to whet your appetite, sir.
A glass, you say? It's an empty little house,
but for last year's brew –
if you're willing to knock back a glass
with the old geezer that lives next door, though,
I'll call him in across the fence,
and we'll drink our fill together.

Staunin Ma Lane

hyne awa i the lift, an eagle hings
inben the braes, a pair o pickie-maas
scovin an tovin, handie for the onding
dandie an cantie, playin back an forrit
the gress wi dew is fair droukit yit
the ettercap's wab still no soupit awa
providence is neaurhaun by aa the warks o man
A staun ma lane, hertsair wi monie sorras

獨立

空外一鷙鳥
河間雙白鷗
飄颻搏擊便
容易往來游
草露亦多濕
蛛絲仍未收
天機近人事
獨立萬端憂

Standing Alone

High in the sky an eagle hangs;
within the valley slopes, a pair of terns.
They play around, open to any attack,
and fly to and fro at their ease.
The grass is still drenched in dew,
the spider's web unbroken;
heaven is close to the affairs of men:
I stand alone, heart-sore with many sorrows.

春望

國破山河在
城春草木深
感時花濺淚
恨別鳥驚心
烽火連三月
家書抵萬金
白頭搔更短
渾欲不勝簪

Vizzy i the Spring

the kinrik's by wi't, but our land's ti the fore still;
the Toun, this spring, is aa growthie wi weeds:
in times like the nou, our blossoms are jawpit wi tears
an birds breinge in on the sorra o our pairtins.
beacon fires hae bleized in spring efter spring:
the ae note frae hame, A'd pey thousans for.
ma lyart hair I've scartit that thin, sae's
muckle tho A ettle at it, it winna haud ma hatpreen.

Survey, in the Spring

The kingdom's wrecked, but our land is still full of life;
the City, this spring, is overgrown with weeds:
at times like these, tears spatter our blossoms,
and birds burst in on the sorrows of parting.
Beacon fires have blazed through spring after spring:
I'd pay thousands for a single note from home.
My greying hair I've scratched so thin, that
however much I try, it will not hold my hatpin.

Frae the Hairt, Traivellin　　　　　　　　旅夜書懷

　　on the haugh fine gress an a smaa wund　　細草微風岸
　on ma boatie a hie-tiltit stang an lanesome nichts　危墻獨夜舟
　　the staurs hingin owre the even outland's braid　星垂平野闊
　an the muin wallachin whaur the Lang Watter jows　月涌大江流
　　　whit wey 'll letters e'er mak ma name?　名豈文章著
　　　A'm auld an seik an shuirlie sud reteir　官應老病休
　　whit am A like, fleein an flichterin about?　飄飄何所似
　　　a pickie-maa, atween the yirth an lift!　天地一沙鷗

From the Heart, Travelling

　　On the river bank fine grass and a light breeze,
　　　on my boat a tall mast and lonely nights;
　the stars hanging over the level breadth of wilderness,
　and the moon wallowing where the Long River swells:
　　　how will writing ever make me famous?
　　　I'm old and ill and should definitely retire.
　　What am I like, rushing pointlessly around?
　　　A seagull, between the earth and sky!

絕句

江邊踏青罷
回首見旌旗
風起春城暮
高樓鼓角悲

Quatrain

on the haughland A step on gress nae mair
turnin about, A spy the airmy pensils flaffin
the wind's risin owre the toun, this nicht o spring
war drums on castle touers – it'll brak yir hairt, this day!

Quatrain

On the riverbank I step on grass no more:
turning around, I see army pennants flapping;
the wind's rising over the town, this night in spring:
war drums on castle towers – it would break your heart, this day!

Spring Sun on the Watterside Clachan

i

Frae toun ti toun, fowk eident at the hairst;
frae bank ti bank, the Watter deep in spate.
Gin A cud see the lang miles o heiven an yirth,
A'd see but the turnin years o aa ma days.
Ma theikit ruif wis warth a pickle poems,
tho in ma hairt it wis Tír na nÓg A socht aye.
Cark an care they smoored the line o ma life –
whit a lang an wearie stravaig ti win here the nou!

ii

Frae hyneawa A cam ti the thrie westlan kinriks:
it wis sax year syne A snappert an fell doun here.
Fremt masel, A forgaither wi auld freins,
but it's burn an shaw that kittles up ma speirits.
That faur ben wi idleset, A'll thole ma dairnit duds,
an whan A gang about, A'll dree ma holie shuin.
Ma mairch fences, they're aathegither stentless,
for the Lang Watter an the lift abune are aa ma joy.

iii

The bamboo A plantit's insnorlt wi tender green,
the geans A sneddit back blushin like wee lassies;
ma hairt clear an cauld as the mune's stane gless,
A'm come to face the wund frae the snawy ben.
An ashet o siller they haunit this auld bodach,
a reid-tape dunderheid at did whit he wis tellt.
An wha wad hae thocht, whan ma teeth hed aa faan out,
ma name'd be set doun i the Buke o Wyce Auld Men?

《春日江村》五首　　　　　　　　　*Spring Sun on the Riverside Village*

一

農務村村急
春流岸岸深
乾坤萬里眼
時序百年心
茅屋還堪賦
桃源自可尋
艱難昧生理
飄泊到如今

　　　　　　　　　　　　　　i

From farm to farm they're busy with their toil;
　　from bank to bank the River's deep in spate.
If I could see the long miles of heaven and earth,
　　I'd see just the turning years of all my days.
My small thatched roof was worth a few poems,
though in my heart I always sought my own Isles of the Blest.
Worry and grief have smothered the lines of my life –
　　what a long weary struggle to get here now!

二

迢遞來三蜀
蹉跎又六年
客身逢故舊
發興自林泉
過懶從衣結
頻游任履穿
藩籬頗無限
恣意向江天

　　　　　　　　　　　　　　ii

From faraway I came to the three kingdoms of the west:
　　it was six years ago I stumbled and fell down here.
A stranger myself, I get together with old friends,
　　but it's streams and woods that lift my spirits.
So far gone in idleness, I'll put up with darned clothes,
　　and when I go walking about, I'll suffer holed shoes.
My boundary fences, they're altogether endless,
　　for the Long River and the sky above are all my joy.

三

種竹交加翠
栽桃爛漫紅
經心石鏡月
到面雪山風
赤管隨王命
銀章付老翁
豈知牙齒落
名玷薦賢中

　　　　　　　　　　　　　　iii

The bamboo bushes I planted are a tangle of tender green;
　　the wild cherries[6] I pruned back blush like little girls;
　　my heart clear and cold as the moon's stone mirror,
I'm come to face the wind from off the snowy mountain.
　　They gave a silver plate to this old geezer,
　　　　an idiot of a time-serving civil servant.
And who'd have thought, when my teeth had all fallen out,
that my name would go down in the Book of Wise Old Men…

---

[6] Naturalized: *peach tree*, in the original.

iv

Maugre ma maladies A hae a crammasy signet still,
but nou A'm hame ti dauner owre purpie crottle;
A'm ettlin at ma eild inben ma kintra yett,
me at wis blate afore the wisocks o the Secretariat.
The bricht leam o the sun twines about the swallas,
an leafs on the watter pairt for the pickie-maas;
whiles the neibours brings shell-puddocks an fishies,
an speir whit time will A can gang an see them.

v

Yin cantin gowk made mane at cateran bands,
the ither wis incaa'd ti Court, a mid-age man;
the tane begoud ti scrieve his *Speil the Touer*,
the tither, weill-infitten, gat glorie for *Bogle Tales*:
their haas hereawa is set doun in the *Buke o Warthies*,
their hie ingyne better-kent nor our Halie Hermits.
In anither season, A umbethocht me o thir twae –
i the sun o yin mair springtime, ma hairt is wae.

四

扶病垂朱紱
歸休步紫苔
郊扉存晚計
幕府愧群材
燕外晴絲卷
鷗邊水葉開
鄰家送魚鱉
問我數能來

五

群盜哀王粲
中年召賈生
登樓初有作
前席竟為榮
宅入先賢傳
才高處士名
異時懷二子
春日復含情

iv

In spite of all my maladies I hold an official signet still,
but wander over the purple lichens, now that I've come home;
I'm planning for old age, within my country gate,
where once I was bashful before the geniuses of the Secretariat.
The bright rays of the sun entwine about the swallows,
and leaves on the river are parted by seagulls;
sometimes my neighbours bring turtles and fishes,
asking when can I go and visit them.

v

One fool[7] made a lament about outlaw bands,
another[8] was summoned to Court, a middle-aged man;
the one began to write *Clamber Up the Tower*,
the other was promoted to glory for his *Ghost Stories*:
their houses were set down in *The Book of Worthies*,
their genius better known than that of our holy Hermits.
In another season, I thought of those two –
in the sun of another springtime, my heart is full of woe.

---

[7] Wang Can (AD 177-217)
[8] Jia Yi (201-169 BC)

The Birslin Sun in Ma Westlin Chaumer

Whan derk winter's happit wi nitherin cauld,
for beikin in the sun, A dearlie lou ma hie touer.
Favour flows doun frae the sun in its auld hame,
wi blusterie Boreas owre blate ti win inben.
Baith birse an hair lies cozie and bien,
an stowlins ma skin feels aa new-wuishen.
The sun's benignitie nae dout rins sae deep
at decrescent vapours is instanter exemit.
A lean masel back, doverin een stellit ti the lift,
the better ti let ma sair feet mend.
Puggies stravaig ramstam about the rammel
as grues tove braw-like owre the brou o the ben.
Freins ken fine the doul of trystin an twynin,
days o gledness an gall gey near dune;
o thir praisent times a rhyme or twa A'll can mak,
tho in a blink ma lifetime o days seems but yestreen.
Langsyne forgaithert wi hairtscaud an wanchance,
the sapient an wyce wi dolour wir forfochen:
whit for sud A uise the gloamin of ma years
ti murn the times, when gane is aa ma sap an fushion?

西閣曝日

The Scorching Sun in My Western Chamber

凜冽倦玄冬
負暄嗜飛閣
羲和流德澤
顒頊愧倚薄
毛髮具自和
肌膚潛沃若
太陽信深仁
衰氣欻有托
攲傾煩注眼
容易收病腳
流離木杪猿
翩躚山顛鶴
用知苦聚散
哀樂日已作
即事會賦詩
人生忽如昨
古來遭喪亂
賢圣盡蕭索
胡為將暮年
憂世心力弱

When dark winter is wrapped in shivering cold,
for basking in the sun, I dearly love my high tower.
Favour flows down from the sun in its old home,
with blustery Boreas too bashful to reach inside.
Both beard and hair lie cosy and comfortable,
and gradually my skin feels all newly-washed.
The sun's magnanimity no doubt runs so deep
that enfeebling vapours instantly evaporate.
I lean back, sleepy eyes fixed on the sky,
the better to let my sore feet rest.
Gibbons roam unrestrained in the branches,
as cranes soar beautifully over the brow of the hill.
Friends know well the sorrow of meeting and parting,
days of gladness and gall almost done;
I can make a rhyme or two on these present times,
though a lifetime suddenly seems like one single day.
Long ago, accompanied by sorrow and bad luck,
sagacious and wise men were worn out by their suffering:
why should I use the twilight of my years to mourn the world's state,
when I am weakened and weary in mind and bodily strength?

No Leavin Ma Westlin Chaumer

i

On the Lang Watter the sauchs is untimeously brairdin
watterside flouers aa rankit pale an wan.
Hereawa the lan sud hae foustie airs an stechie,
but this year-en it hauds the firstlins o the ware.
Ma leir's aa tint, an me turnt donnert an doitit,
wi nae ither kin, A'm thrang wi ma ain auld sel.
An the Westlin Chaumer's souch A'd niver kent,
gin ance A thocht ti gang, cud it kep uis back?

ii

Tho the Westlin Chaumer wad lea a bodie gang,
this bodie the day wad willintlie stop for aye.
Abune the Lang Watter it's aa clouds o whitest silk,
an the Waa o Stanes is threwn aa owre wi emerant;
the faemie sea'll fu air the sun convoy,
or the White Strip'll be strinklit owre wi sternies.
Ma haill life lang A've loued the bonnie an the braw –
an, whow me, for a wunner, nou A've fund it!

不離西閣

Not Leaving My Western Chamber

一

江柳非時發
江花冷色頻
地偏應有瘴
臘近已含春
失學從愚子
無家住老身
不知西閣意
肯別定留人

i

On the Long River the willows are coming untimely into leaf,
ranks of riverside flowers are pale and cold-looking.
Hereabouts the land should be putting forth pestilential miasmas,
but so near the end of this year it's showing the first signs of spring.
My learning's all lost, and I've become wandered in my wits,
with no relatives, I'm busy with just my own old self.
Suppose I'd never known the Western Chamber's style,
had I thought to leave, would it have held me back?

二

西閣從人別
人今亦故亭
江雲飄素練
石壁斷空青
滄海先迎日
銀河倒列星
平生耽勝事
吁駭始初經

ii

Even if the Western Chamber would let a person go,
today this man would willingly stay for ever.
Above the Long River it's all clouds of whitest silk,
and the Wall of Stones is broken up by green malachite;
the foamy sea will early accompany the sun,
or the Milky Way be sprinkled all over with stars.
My whole life long, I've loved the beautiful and the fine –
And what a wonder it is that I've found it now!

Hairst-Time Quicknin

1

Nithert bi the dews o the hairst time,
    the maple shaws are dwynin;
on the Carlin Hills an Carlin's Cleuch
    the air's caller an cauld.
The Muckle Watter's gowstie jows
    are lowpin e'en ti the lift,
an outowre the border the derk-like yird
    convoys the drumlie clouds.
Chrysanths – twice ti ma ee they bring
    tears for ither days.
Yon coble tethert its leesome lane,
    it's me ettlin for ma kailyaird.
The winter duds is out in ilka airt,
    an fowk eidently cloutin them:
hie abune White Imperatour toun,
    claes-bittles thrang in the gloamin.

秋興八首

一

玉露凋傷楓樹林
巫山巫峽氣蕭森
江間波浪兼天湧
塞上風雲接地陰
叢菊兩開他日淚
孤舟一系故園心
寒衣處處催刀尺
白帝城高急暮砧

Autumn Quickening

1

Shivered by the dews of harvest time,
    the maple woods are fading;
on the Carlin Hills and Carlin's Gorge
    the air is keen and cold.
The Long Water's gusty waves
    are leaping high aloft,
and out beyond the border
the dark land connects with troubled clouds.
Chrysanthemums – twice to my eye
    they've brought tears for other days.
A skiff all by itself
    ties my heart to my own old garden.
Winter clothes are out in every part,
    and people diligently beating them:
high above White Imperator town,
    clothes-beetles busy in the gloaming.

2

The sklentin sun is faain fast
on this lanefu southron toun;
Whane'er the sterns o the Plew comes out,
A turn ti the Citie o Peace.
A lissen ti the puggies yowl-yowlin awa:
thrie times they sab, in suith!
An here's me, chairgt wi a yuiseless eerant,
a raft in the back-en o the year.
Frae decorit chancellery and perfumit incenser
A'm banist, prostrait on ma bowster,
as inben the hill biggins' caukit bittlins,
dowie whissles cry their dool.
Oh sirs, see ye on yonder stanes
the mune throu aa the speilin-leaf!
She's aye been leamin on the rashie-flouers
aa alang the annays!

二

夔府孤城落日斜
每依南斗望京華
聽猿實下三聲淚
奉使虛隨八月槎
畫省香爐違伏枕
山樓粉堞隱悲笳
請看石上藤蘿月
已映洲前蘆荻花

2

The slanting sun is falling fast
on this lonely southern town[9];
whenever the stars of the Plough come out,
I turn to the City of Peace[10].
I listen to the gibbons wail:
they really do sob three times!
And here I am, charged with a useless errand,
a raft in the autumn of the year.
From decorated chancellery and perfumed incense burner
I'm banished, prostrate on my pillow,
as inside the hill buildings' chalk-white battlements,
doleful whistles cry their woe.
Oh sirs, see on yonder stones
the moon through all the creepers!
She's been shining on the bulrushes
all along the river islands!

---

[9] Kuizhou
[10] Chang'an

3

A thousan hames in the hilltoun there,
    beikin lown in the sun;
      day an daily in ma watterside touer
    A sit mang rouks an drows.
    Fishin fowk, twa nichts awa
      come efter ither hame,
an swallas in the clear an caller hairst
      flichter an flee about.
    Kuang Heng monisht his king,
      his fame wis niver muckle;
Liu Xiang exponit the Canonicals,
      his hert's wishes wir fichlt.
Schuil friens, the billies o ma youthheid,
      monie's daein weill,
wi jauds o the sonsiest, claes o the best,
    an braw houses on the hill.

三

千家山郭靜朝暉
日日江樓坐翠微
信宿漁人還泛泛
清秋燕子故飛飛
匡衡抗疏功名薄
劉向傳經心事違
同學少年多不賤
五陵裘馬自輕肥

3

A thousand homes in the hill town there,
    quietly bask in the sun;
      daily in my waterside tower
    I sit among mist and rain.
    Fishing folk, two nights away,
      come one after the other home,
and swallows in the clear fresh autumn
      flutter and fly about.
    Kuang Heng admonished his king,
      his fame was never great;
Liu Xiang expounded the Canon,
      his heart's wishes were frustrated.[11]
School friends, the pals of my youth:
      many are doing well,
with well-fed mounts, clothes of the best,
    and fine houses on the hill.

---

[11] Kuang Heng (fl. 43BC) and Liu Xiang (79-8BC) were both Han dynasty scholars.

4

A've heard them say the Citie o Peace,
it's awfu like a dambrod:
this hunner year, o Affairs o State –
naethin bar dule an sorra.
Palaces an pleasances o kings an princes,
they've aa new lairdies nou;
crouns an coats for Policy an Weir,
they're no like hou they wir.
Ance northawa owre ben an swyre
gowden drums wad be dirlin,
an westawa mang airmy cairts
post-riders wad gae birlin.
Dragons an fishies are lanesome an eerie
for in hairst, the Watter's freezin:
ti see ma land lythe an lown,
it's efter that A'm greinin.

四

聞道長安似弈棋
百年世事不勝悲
王侯第宅皆新主
文武衣冠異昔時
直北關山金鼓震
征西車馬羽書遲
魚龍寂寞秋江冷
故國平居有所思

4

I've heard them say the City of Peace
is very like a chessboard:
these hundred years, of Affairs of State –
nothing but pain and sorrow.
Palaces and pleasances of kings and princes,
they've all new landlords now;
crowns and coats for officials of Policy and War,
they're not what they used to be.
Once northward over mountain and pass
golden drums would be thrilling,
and westward among army carts
post-riders would go speeding.
Dragons and fish are lonely and strange
for in autumn, the Water's freezing:
to see my land quiet and at peace,
it's after that I'm yearning.

5

The ports o Paradise Palace staun
  forenent the Southron Hills;
The Gowden Stoup ingaithers dew
  frae out the Milky Strip.
Westawa A'd watch the Linns o Jade,
  the Mither Queen descendin;
Eastawa, the Auld Ane's purpie lowe,
  the Cadget Swyre stowin.
The clouds wad pairt an the faisants' tails
  apen the palace yett;
an the sun's retour ti the dragon scales
  wad lat ken the face o Majestie.
Doverin ma lane abune the lang watter,
  A wunner at anither hairst:
monie's the time wi ma chein o jade
  A've stuid rankit in the dawin.

五

蓬萊宮闕對南山
承露金莖霄漢間
西望瑤池降王母
東來紫氣滿函關
雲移雉尾開宮扇
日繞龍鱗識聖顏
一臥滄江驚歲晚
幾回青瑣點朝班

5[12]

The gates of Paradise Palace
stand before the Southern Hills; the Golden Pillar gathers the dew
down from the Milky Way.
Westward I'd watch the Falls of Jade,
the Mother Queen descending;
Eastward, the Old One's purple glow, the Casket Pass enfolding.
The clouds would part and the pheasants' tails
open the palace door;
the sun's return to the dragon scales
would make known the face of Majesty.
Dozing alone above the Long Water,
I wonder at another autumn:
many's the time with my chain of jade
I've stood in line at the dawning.[13]

---

[12] References to the Citie o Peace (Chang'an), its sights and its surroundings. *The Auld Ane* is a literal translation of Laozi, who is said to have dictated the *Dao De Jing* on Cadget Swyre, above the Yellow River. Supernatural manifestations are marked by a purple haze.

[13] That is, as a high official at the Royal Levée, which took place at first light.

6

Owre bi Hernstank Cleuch mou
an the heid o the Quave Watter,
a thousand mile o tovin smeik,
aa the dowie hairst.
Throu Calyx Haa athort the barmkin,
comes the Royal Ridin,
ti Smaa Hibiscus Green He'll gae,
ti hear the sorras o the Border.
Hingins o the pearl an browdert stoups
umbeset wi yalla cranes;
bawdkin tows an masts o the ivory,
white maas munt abune them.
Leukin back, A murn yon airt
o singin an o dancing,
this land o ours, at ance langsyne
wis aye the Land o Kings.

六

瞿塘峽口曲江頭
萬裏風煙接素秋
花蕚夾城通禦氣
芙蓉小苑入邊愁
珠簾繡柱圍黃鵠
錦纜牙牆起白鷗
回首可憐歌舞地
秦中自古帝王州

6

Over by the mouth of Cranepool Gorge
and the head of the Winding River,
a thousand miles of blowing smoke,
all the doleful autumn.
Through Calyx Hall athwart the barmkin
comes the Royal Riding,
to Small Hibiscus Green He'll go,
to hear the sorrows of the Border.
Hangings of pearl and embroidered pillars
set about with yellow cranes;
brocade ropes and masts of ivory,
white gulls mounting above them.
Looking back, I mourn that place
of singing and of dancing,
this land of ours, that long ago
was always the Land of Kings.

7

The watters o Britherbricht Loch wis brocht
bi the langsyne Hous o Han:
His Martial Majestie's pinnets an pensils –
they're here afore our een.
Tuim is the Weaver Lassie's lume,
this nicht ablow the mune;
the shelly-coat on the stane Sea-Baist
wags in the hairst wund.
In the loch's sweel an swaa the zizanie,
a derklike cloud, is sunken;
in the cauld dew, frae nenuphars
the reid pouther's faain.
Hie's the swyres, ti the lift abune,
a gate juist birds can gang:
lochs an wattersides ti the warld's en,
an yin auld bodach, fishin.

七

昆明池水漢時功
武帝旌旗在眼中
織女機絲虛夜月
石鯨鱗甲動秋風
波漂菰米沉雲黑
露冷蓮房墜粉紅
關塞極天惟鳥道
江湖滿地一漁翁

7

The waters of Brotherbright Lake were brought
by the long-ago Dynasty of Han:
His Martial Majesty's pennants and streamers,[14]
they're here before our eyes.
Empty is the Weaver Girl's loom,
tonight below the moon;
the coat of shells on the stone Sea-Beast[15]
wags in the autumn wind.
In the lake's ebb and flow the zizanie,
a dark cloud, is sunken;
in the cold dew, from nenuphars
the red pollen is falling.
High are the passes, to the heavens above,
a road only birds can go:
lakes and riverbanks to the world's end,
and one old chap, fishing.

[14] i.e. Emperor Wu Di (156-87BC) of the Han Dynasty.
[15] Two famous statues in the capital, the Herd Lad and the Weaver Lassie – mythical lovers – they stood by Britherbricht Loch, as did another famous statue of a sea monster.

8

Frae Brithermine Shiels ti Kingspairk Burn,
yon lang an wimpling gate,
whaur the Kip o Purpieport's shedda
faas inti the Pirlin Pule,
the sweet-rice shanks is etten awa,
taen for vivers ti papingos,
an planetree beuchs hae auldlike grown
whaur ance the phenix reistit.
For kingfisher feathers the lassies forgaithert
an A wad salute them in the spring;
or, immortal feres in our boatie thegither,
we'd set our sail at e'en.
A'd tak a pen in times bypast,
an A'd scrieve thae things ti the life –
white o the pow, A sang o the Citie:
nou sorra bous ma heid.

八

昆吾御宿自逶迤
紫閣峰陰入美陂
香稻啄餘鸚鵡粒
碧梧棲老鳳凰枝
佳人拾翠春相問
仙侶同舟晚更移
彩筆昔曾幹氣象
白頭吟望苦低垂

8

From Brothermine Shiels to Kingspark Stream,
that long and winding road,
where the Purpleport Peak's shadow
falls into the Rippling Pool,
the sweet-rice stalks are all eaten up,
taken as food for parrots,
and sycamore boughs have grown old,
where once the phoenix roosted.
For kingfisher feathers the girls gathered,
and I would salute them in the spring;
immortal companions in our boat together,
we'd set our sail at evening.
I'd take my pen in times long past,
and describe these things to the life.
White-haired, once I sang the City:
now I bow my head in sorrow.

The Banished Immortal

謫仙人

Li Bai

李白

Li Bai (701-762), is always paired with his younger contemporary Du Fu, the exuberant, swashbuckling Taoist Yang to Du Fu's sober, engaged, compassionate Confucian Yin. He may have been of non-Chinese extraction, perhaps of Central Asian Turkic descent, and he claimed to have been a wandering swordsman in his youth. He was famous for his armed chivalry, his public drunkenness, his disdain for etiquette, and his hard-living style. He was also a great wanderer and a mountain climber; his poetry exults over the wonders of nature, the joys of friendship, the ephemeral nature of human life, dream-like shamanic rapture, and the pleasures of wine. (Grape wine from Central Asia was fashionable in his day, as against the rice beers that would have been more traditional – and which are still widely drunk today.)

He was famous in his own time, and is widely known in the West as Li Po. (Po, or nowadays, Bo, is the old-fashioned polite reading of his personal name.) He was traditionally said to have drowned one night, as, drunk on a boat, he reached out to grab the moon on the water, but it is more likely that he died of natural causes: some have speculated that he died of tuberculosis, and others that he died of drink.

Bring the Bevvy Ben

Och sirs, hae ye no seen the muckle Yalla Watter
Gae rowin doun ti the sea, comin back never?

Och sirs, hae ye no seen the keekin-glesses in the bricht haa,
Ruein this mornin's jet-black hair, that's nou as white as snaa?

In this life, gin richt vogie ye wad be, man,
Dinna lea yir gowden tassie tuim ablow the mune!

A uised ma hie ingyne frae Heiven Abune:
Thousans in gowd A've spent, that'll no come back sune.

Roast ye yowes an slauchter nowt for grand fun:
It'll tak three hunner drams ti mak ae sederunt!

Be ye auld bodach or be ye bold callant –
Bring the bevvy ben, an keep it comin!

A'll sing ye a sang, sirs, an it please ye,
Sae len uis yir lugs, and tak tent o me:

Whit's the avail o yir utter-fine quaich, yir gemstane?
Aa ye want's ti be forever fou, an ne'er be fresh again!

The langsyne saints an sages wir torn-faced, ilka ane:
Forbye the drinkers, there's nae ithers left a guid name.

The King o Chen rantit throu The Peacefu Pleasance,
Reid-wud for pleisur, pourin drams bi the millions.

李白
將進酒

君不見
黃河之水天上來，奔流到海不復回？
君不見
高堂明鏡悲白髮，朝如青絲暮成雪？
人生得意須盡歡，莫使金樽空對月。
天生我材必有用，千金散盡還復來。
烹羊宰牛且為樂，會須一飲三百杯。
岑夫子，丹丘生，
將進酒，君莫停。
與君歌一曲，請君為我側耳聽。
鐘鼓饌玉不足貴，但願長醉不願醒。
古來聖賢皆寂寞，惟有飲者留其名。
陳王昔時宴平樂，鬥酒十千恣歡謔。
主人何為言少錢，逕須沽取對君酌。
五花馬，千金裘，
呼兒將出換美酒，與爾同銷萬古愁！

Bring in the Booze

Oh sirs, have you never seen the great Yellow River
Go rolling down to the sea, coming back never?

Oh sirs, have you never seen the mirrors in the bright hall,
Ruing this morning's black hair, that's now as white as snow?

In this life, if you'd do it stylishly, man,
Don't leave your golden goblet empty beneath the moon!

I used my great intelligence from Heaven Above:
Thousands in gold I've spent, that won't come back soon.

Roast ewes and slaughter cattle for big fun:
It'll take three hundred glasses to make one proper sitting!

Be you old geezer or be you bold young gallant
Bring in the booze, and keep it coming!

I'll sing you a song, sirs, if it pleases you,
So lend me your ears and take notice of me:

What's your precious silver cups, your gemstones worth?
All you want is to be forever sloshed, and never sober again!

Saints and sages on the past were glum and gloomy every one:
Except for the drinkers, no others left behind a good name.

The King of Chen ranted through the Peaceful Pleasance,
Pure mad for pleasure, pouring drinks by the millions.

Guidman, whit dae ye mean, ye're short o siller?
A'll get a roun in, sir, an drink wi ye instanter:

Ma pyot naigie, ma costly sable coatie –
Gar the boy lay them in wad for a swallie,
An thegither we'll gar lang ages o dule
      saunt clean awa!

Landlord, what do you mean, ye're short of money?
I'll buy a round and drink with you right away:

My brindled horse, my costly sable mantle –
Get the boy to pawn them for a few drinks,
And together we'll make long ages of woe
       vanish clean away!

The Dream Talisman
夢符

Qiao Ji (c.1280-1345)
喬吉

Qiao Ji (c.1280-1345), also known as Qiao Jifu, whose courtesy name *Mengfu* means *Dream Talisman*, was one of the most famous dramatists of the Yuan Dynasty, when China was part of the Mongol Empire and literati like him were all but debarred from holding office as mandarins, the career for which they had spent a lifetime training. Like many another, he seems to have drifted into the entertainment quarter of his adopted home, Hangzhou, and to have devoted himself to the theatre. Many of his poems survive, and are unusually frank by Chinese standards in their depiction of romantic and sexual love. He seems to have been deeply in love with Li Chuyi, a singing girl from Yangzhou who was bought or otherwise taken away from him by a rich and powerful mandarin: she appears in many of his poems, as does his open declaration that his heart was broken by the experience.

Only three of his plays survive, but we have eleven of his long poem cycles and over two hundred short poems.

Shuitin Geese

i

ti the southron air *Liangzhou No. 7*

Reid fishtails haurdlie kythin i the failin dawin rouk,
green deuks' heids on the wimplin hairst-time waters,
skyrie hibiscus dancin abune the pirlin o the pule;
a pair o pickie-maas, see, joukin an divin,
fishie-boats comin an gaun,
withert gress on the links,
grey haar on auld trees.
Hairtsome, lousome, the waterside clachan:
e'en wi a skeilly brush o reids an greens ye cudna shaw it.
Dicht on indigo for the burn, tho,
spread pouther about for white duckweed on the watter-lip,
rub in rouge for the reid wuids afore ye.

A rowed up the brim o ma rashie-bunnet,
raised up ma heid,
liftit ma een,
got a glisk o a line o wild geese i the lift
screivin out letters on the lucky clouds,
birlin slaw an slaw richt abune ma heid.

梁州第七・射雁

Shooting Geese

i
to the southern-style air *Liangzhou No. 7*

魚尾紅殘霞隱隱
鴨頭綠秋水涓涓
芙蓉燦爛搖波面
見沉浮鷗伴
來往魚船
平沙衰草
古木蒼煙
江鄉景堪愛堪憐
有丹青巧筆難傳
揉藍靛綠水溪頭
鋪膩粉白蘋岸邊
抹胭脂紅葉林前
將笠檐兒慢卷
迎頭
仰面
偷晴兒覷見碧天外雁行現
寫破祥雲一片箋
頭直上慢慢盤旋

Red fishtails hardly visible in the fading mist of dawn,
green ducks' heads on the whirling autumn waters,
bright hibiscus dancing above the rippling of the pool;
a pair of gulls, see, ducking and diving,
fishing boats coming and going,
withered grass on the links,
a grey mist on the old trees.
How delightful, how endearing the riverside village is;
even with a skilled brush of colours you couldn't show it.
But dab on indigo for the stream,
spread face powder for the white duckweed on the banks,
and rub on rouge for the red woods before you.
I rolled up the brim of my straw hat,
raised my head,
lifted my eyes,
got a glimpse of a line of wild geese in the sky
spelling out letters on the lucky clouds,
spinning slowly right above my head.

Shuitin Geese

ii

ti the air *The Flourishin Brainch*

A pickt my pyot-paintit bou up richt quick,
tuik ma eagle-feather arras speedily,
strauchtent out ma swalla-tail arra heids in nae time,
hankit on ma tiger-thairm boustring.
Bou as roun as the hairst mune,
arra strecht as the levin's flicht,
heich-awa A vizzied, naethin ajee,
an shot a passin swan fairly:
it fell in the rashes an A lost it.

一枝花

忙拈鵲畫弓
急取雕翎箭
端直了燕尾鶬
搭上虎筋弦
秋月弓圓
箭發如飛電
覷高低無側偏
正中賓鴻
落在蒹葭不見

Shooting Geese

ii

to the air *The Flowering Branch*

I swiftly picked up my magpie-painted bow,
rapidly got out my eagle-feather arrows,
straightened out my swallowtail arrowheads in no time,
hooked up my tiger-gut bowstring.
Bow round as the harvest moon,
arrow straight as the lightning's strike,
I sighted away up high, dead centre,
and shot a passing swan:
it fell in the rushes and I lost it.

Shuitin Geese
iii
Coda

尾

轉過紫荊坡白草冢黃蘆堰
驚起些紅腳鴨金頭鵝錦背鴛
嚇得這鸂鶒兒連忙向敗荷里串
血模糊翅搧扇
撲剌剌可憐
十二枝梢翎向地皮上剪

Throu reid-brierie scaurs, white weedie tombs an yalla-rashie sheuchs A gaed,
reid-fuit deuks, gowden-heidit geese an brocade-backit deuks A stertlt,
scared fewlums in flochts straucht ti withert lillie-beds.

Bluid blurred its beatin wings:
a peitifu flichterin.
A dizzen brainch-ens cuttit wi its faa

Shooting Geese
iii
Coda

By red-briar slopes, white weedy tombs and ditches of yellow rushes I went,
red-footed ducks, golden-headed geese and brocade-back ducks I startled,
scared flocks of water-birds[18] into beds of withered waterlilies.
Blood blurred its beating wings:
a pitiful fluttering,
a dozen branches broken by its fall.

---

[18] The sole source for *fewlum*, a very obscure term for a bird – a genuine *hapax legomenon*, in fact – is *He comptis na mair the gled than the fewlume*, Gawain Douglas *Aeneid* ix. Prol. 47. (DSL s.v. *fewlume*). The Chinese term is of equally baffling obscurity. The largest and most specialised dictionaries tell us no more than 'a water-bird, bigger than a duck' or 'a water-bird, possibly purple'.

Pairtin Luve

喬牌兒·別情

i

ti the air *Pauchlin at the Cairds*

The Phoenix Seeks its Marra
harpin on a slaw air;
The Oreole Seeks its Maik –
dinna sing yon sang.
The *Deas o the Sun* cuttit aff aathegither
frae the *Lether til the Cairrie*,
an *Peach Flouer Glen* is awa
whaur *Westlin Roads is Dour*.

鳳求凰琴慢彈
鶯求友曲休咀
楚陽臺更隔著連雲棧
桃源洞在蜀道難

Parting Love[19]

i

to the air *Cheating at Cards*

The Phoenix Seeks its Consort, harping on some old slow air;
The Oriole Seeks its Mate – don't sing that song.
The *Sun's Stand* is cut off altogether from the *Ladder to the Sky*,
and *Peach Blossom Valley* is far away where *Western Roads are Hard*.

---

[19] Italics = song titles. *Deas o the Sun* and *Peach Flouer Glen* are connotated with the highly desirable state of living at ease on an official salary, while *Lether til the Cairrie* and *Westlin Roads is Dour* hint at the hard work involved in passing the official examinations that gave entry to the mandarinate. *The Phoenix Seeks its Marra* and *The Oriole Seeks its Maik* tells us he isn't lucky in love either.

攬箏琶

無邊岸
黑海也似那煎煩
愁萬結柔腸
淚雙垂業眼
淚眼與愁腸
直熬得燭滅香殘
更闌
望情人必然來夢間
爭奈這枕冷衾寒

Parting Love

ii
to the air *Fiddling with the Harp*

No end to it, no shore:
sore grief like a black sea.
Sorrow ties my guts into a thousand knots,
Doubled tears in my wicked eyes.
Tears in my eyes, sorrow in my guts,
the dying flame and the failing incense still to endure.
In the small hours,
waiting for my love (surely she'll come into my dreams?)
how can I bear the cold pillow, the chilly bedclothes?

Pairtin Luve

ii
ti the air *Poukin at the Clarsach*

Nae en ti't, nae shore:
sair hairt-scauds
like a bleck sea.
Sorra thraws ma wame
inti a thousan knots,
doublt tears
in ma ill-daein een.
Tears i the een,
sorra i the wame,
the deein flame
an dwynin incense
still ti thole.
I the wee hours
waitin on ma luve
(shuirlie she'll come
inti ma dreams?)
Hou'll A can staun
the cauld cod,
the wearie covers?

Pairtin Luve　　　　　　　　　落梅風

iii
ti the air *Plum Blossom Souch*

Fouterin wi her dulcimer,
derk flauchts o hair letten doun –
never eident wi her leuks, A mind –
luve's langsyne turnt her ti idleset:
naither kaimed nor pouthert,
but bonnie ti see –
her naitral sel.

粘金雁
斡翠鬟
想不曾做心兒打扮
近新來為咱情緒懶
不梳妝也自然好看

Parting Love

iii
to the air *Plum Blossom Breeze*

Fiddling with her dulcimer,
dark locks of hair let down –
never one to bother with her looks, I remember –
love has long since made her lazy:
neither combed nor made-up, but lovely to look at – her natural self.

沉醉東風

風鈴響猛猜做佩環
柳煙顰只疑是眉攢
想犀梳似新月牙
憶宮額似芙蓉瓣
見桃花呵似見他容顏
覷得越女吳姬匹似閑
厭聽那銀箏象板

Parting Love

iv

to the air *Drunk on the East Wind*

Bells on the wind, and I think of bracelets,
two willows drooping in the mist – is it her frown?
Her ivory comb, the new moon's horn,
her brow, I remember, white as a lily;
peach blossom, oh, it's the colour of her cheeks.
Women from the east, southern lasses, they're nice enough to look at,
but their silver dulcimers and their ivory castanets have sickened me.

Pairtin Luve

iv
ti the air *Fou wi the Eastlin Wund*

Bells on the wind,
A think on bracelets.
twa sauchtrees hing i the haar,
is't her froun?
Her ivorie kaim,
The new mune's horn;
Her brou, A mind,
a lilly-flouer;
The peachtree's flourish,
Och, it's like her cheek.

Weimen o the east,
southron lassies,
they're braw eneuch ti see,
but their ivorie clappers,
their siller dulcimers –
they've scunnert me.

93

Pairtin Luve

本調煞

v

Coda, Diminuendo

A'm gyte gane wi luve:
whan'll A be easy in masel?
Mairatowre,
A'm feelin that forhooiet,
naither bite nor sup A pree.
It's aa ti thole yet –
the seas gaun dry,
rocks meltin wi the sun.

相思成病何時慢
更拚得不茶不飯
直熬個海枯石爛

Parting Love

v

Coda, Diminuendo

I've gone crazy for love: when will I be myself again?
And on top of that, I feel so forsaken, I can neither eat nor drink.
It's all to be endured – the seas going dry, the rocks melting in the sun.[20]

---

[20] Yes, indeed, and Qiao Ji wasn't the first to use these images, either: a song survives from the 10th or 11th century which also prefigures Robert Burns in exactly the same words.

憑欄人・春思

淡月梨花曲檻傍
清露蒼苔羅襪涼
　恨他愁斷腸
　為他燒夜香

Greinin for Luve

ti the air *She's Hingin Owre the Palins*

Ablow a pale mune,
peartree flourish
rins inlang the palins.
Caller dew on blae moss,
cauld on stockins o gauze:
missin him, ma hairt braks for sorra.

Up the hail nicht,
burnin incense
for the sake o him.

Yearning for Love

to the air *She's Leaning on the Railings*

Below a pale moon, pear blossom lines the curving fences.
Fresh dew on livid blue-green moss, cold on stockings of gauze:
missing him, my heart is breaking with sorrow.
Up the whole night, burning incense for him.

Speakin o Masel

ti the air *Green Sauchs*

A niver ettlt ti be the Dux,
wis niver in the Buik o Warthie Men:
Sanct o the Dram
onietime,
Precentor o Poetry
oniewhaur,
Tap o the Cless
for haars an dawin clouds,
Drucken Immortal
o watters an lochsides,
for bletherin an lauchin
A sud be
Compiler ti the Faculty.

A stickit sage, for fortie year
A scrievit on the wind
an dichtit at the mune.

柳梢青・自述

Speaking of Myself

to the air *Green Willows*[21]

不占龍頭選
不入名賢傳
時時酒圣
處處詩禪
煙霞狀元
江湖醉仙
笑談便是編修院
留連
批風抹月四十年

I never intended to graduate as Primus,
was never in the Book of Worthies:
Saint of the Dram any time,
Cantor of Poetry anywhere,
Top of the Class for the dewy mists and morning clouds of dalliance.
Drunken Immortal of the highways and byways,
For talking nonsense and laughs, I should be Compiler to the Faculty.
A sage who never graduated,
for forty years I wrote light verse and chased after pleasure.

---

[21] Alternative title instead of *A Wastrie o Green/Extravagance of Green*

At Thornieburn

ti the air *Poukin the Cannel*

A speir at the houses
on Thornieburn side,
whae's aucht them?
Nae ploums plantit,
auld trees haudin up the yetts,
wild rashes taiglin the bankins,
withert bamboo smooring the palins:
an abbey wi nae freirs,
sclaits rummelt wi the tods;
a court wi nae pleas,
bleck rottans for the macers –
white watter,
yalla saun.

A've leaned owre aa the railins,
An ilka skreichin corbie's
been
countit.

折桂令・荊溪即事

問荊溪溪上人家
為甚人家
不種梅花
老樹支門
荒蒲繞岸
苦竹圈笆
寺無僧狐貍樣瓦
官無事烏鼠當衙
白水黃沙
倚遍欄干
數盡啼鴉

At Thornieburn

to the air *Picking Cassia*

I ask the houses at Thornieburn who owns them?
No plums planted, old trees holding the gates up,
wild rushes tangling the bankings,
withered bamboo smothering the fences:
an abbey with no friars, its slates jumbled by the foxes;
a court with no cases, black rats as its officials –
white water, yellow sand.
I've leaned over all the railings,
and every squawking crow has been counted.

For Hou Suo, at Shaoxing

ti the air *Wee Peach-Flouer Pink*

小桃紅・紹興于侯索賦

Aa the lang day,
idleset amang the law books,
naethin gaun on.
The court's skailt,
an the forenune's no by:
the haill county –
twa thousan lieges –
tells o peace an quiet.
The hairst corn,
the simmer cess,
it's dune in a meenit.

畫長無事簿書閑
未午衙先散
一郡居民二十尤
報平安
秋糧夏稅咄嗟兒辦
執花紋象簡
憑琴堂書案
日日看青山

He gaithers flouers,
scrieves curlicues o wryte,
leans his dulcimer on the office desk,
day an daily looks out owre green green hills.

For Hou Suo, at Shaoxing

to the air *Little Peach-Blossom Pink*

All the long day, idleness among the law books, nothing going on.
The court's dismissed, and the morning's still not over:
the whole county – two thousand lieges –
tells of peace and quiet.
The harvest corn, the summer land-tax, are done in a minute.
He gathers flowers, writes calligraphy,
leans his dulcimer on the office desk,
day after day looks out on green, green hills.

小桃紅・別楚儀

一樽別酒斷腸詞
難說心間事
行李匆匆怎酬志
自尋思
從今別卻文章士
至如小子
十分不是
好處也想些兒

Leavin Ma Dawtie Chuyi

ti the air *Wee Peach-Flouer Pink*

Yin pairtin gless
an a sair sair sang:
whit's in ma hairt canna be tellt.
Ma gear's aa throuither –
whit thenks can A cun ye for aa yir mense?

A think ti masel,
frae this pairtin on,
A'm ti be a prosy scholar,
but A'm liker a wean:
it's wrang, aathegither.
The guid side?
That, A'll hae ti think about…

Leaving My Darling Chuyi

to the air *Little Peach-Blossom Pink*

One parting glass, and a hard song:
what's in my heart can't be told.
My stuff is all in a mess –
what thanks can I give for all your good sense?
I think to myself, from this parting,
I'm to be a prosy scholar,
but I'm more like a child:
it's wrong, altogether.
The good side? That I'll have to think about…

Antrin Thochts

ti the air *Heiven's Undefylit Sauns*

3

Wha wis't neist door
at loued ma lute?
Leanin ahint yir hingins,
ye kent uis bi ma lilt.
Frae then ti this,
ae wurd, nae mair:
in thenks A'll rummle ye
yir waddin quilt,
yir bridal bed.

净沙 · 即事

三

隔窗誰愛聽琴
倚簾人是知音
一句話當時至今
今番推甚
酬勞鳳枕鴛衾

Random Thoughts

to the air *Heaven's Pure Sands*

3

Who was it next door who loved my lute?
Leaning behind your curtain, you knew me by my music.
From then to now, one word, no more:
in thanks I'll rumple your wedding quilt, your bridal bed.

<table>
<tr><td>

天净沙 · 即事

四
鶯鶯燕燕春春
花花柳柳真真
事事風風韻韻
嬌嬌嫩嫩
停停當當人人

</td><td>

Antrin Thochts

ti the air *Heiven's Undefylit Sauns*

4
yalla-yites yalla-yite
swallas swalla
spring springs
flouers flouer
sauchs sauch
true's true
ilka thing ilka thing
style's style
rhyme's rhyme
bonnie's bonnie
lousome's lousome
aabodie aabodie
juist the thing
juist the thing

</td></tr>
</table>

Random Thoughts

to the air *Heaven's Pure Sands*

4
Yellowhammers yellowhammer[22], swallows swallow, spring springs,
flowers flower, willows willow, true's true,
every thing, every thing, style is style, rhyme is rhyme,
bonny is bonny, lovable is lovable,
everybody everybody, just the thing, just the thing.

---

[22] Naturalised: *oriole* in the original.

A Screivit Whit A Spyed

ti the air *Reid Steikit Shune*

A younker's face at canna hide
her birlin heid;
a thin wee fan at winna cut her aff
frae the stushie o the singin.
Lettin on she's reddin up her gowden kaim,
she keeks in hidlins at her jo.

A snell wund sobers up ma boozie een.
The bricht mune skails aa ma musardrie.

A'll no sleep soun this nicht, A dout.

紅繡鞋・書所見

臉兒嫩難藏酒暈
扇兒薄不隔歌塵
伴整金釵暗窺人
　涼風醒醉眼
　明月破詩魂
料今宵怎睡得穩

I Wrote What I Saw

to the air *Red Embroidered Shoes*

Her young and tender face can't hide her spinning head;
Her little fan won't cut her off from the hubbub of the singing.
Pretending to fix her golden comb, she sneaks a look at her lover.
A chill wind sobers up my boozy eyes.
The bright moon dispels my poet's dreams.
I won't sleep sound tonight, I fear.

Fine in Idleset

tii the air *Fankle o Jewellit Rammel*

i

Awa in the hills, ablow the wuids
there's a theikit shed wi rashie windaes,
bieldit, lown an bonnie;
green bamboo, emerant pines –
it's fair a pictur.

Nearhaun by, a reikie fairmtoun
o thrie-fower faimlies;
bonnie dreams come flauchterin doun
wi ilka flouer at faas,
An aa the moniplied warldlie pleisurs,
they're as wersh as chowin wax.

Ma lyart pow's juist sic an sae,
an aa turnt beilin white:
nae guid steirin up the puggie o the mind,
the cuddie o the will.

A pit ma ain marrows in;
A gaither ma ain tea leafs;
on the stove A byle ma ain elixirs:
A'll cun a quair o *The Wey an its Maucht*,
blether a whylie wi poachers or wuidmen,
in idleset steik the yett
o ma hibiscus hedge,
an lie fou ablow ma cucumber frame.

It's pure idleset, aathegither –
an A'm content ayont aa meisur!

106

玉交枝・閑適

一

山間林下
有草舍蓬窗幽雅
蒼松翠竹堪圖畫
近煙村三四家
飄飄好夢隨落花
紛紛世味如嚼蠟
一任他蒼頭皓髮
莫徒勞心猿意馬
自種瓜
自采茶
爐內鏈丹砂
看一卷道德經
講一會漁樵話
閉上槿樹籬
醉臥在葫蘆架
盡清閑自在煞

Contented in Idleness

to the air *Tangle of Jade Branches*

1

Away in the hills, below the woods
there's a thatched shed with rush windows, sheltered, snug and bonny;
green bamboo, emerald pines – it's quite the pretty picture.
Nearby, the smoke from a hamlet of three or four families:
sweet dreams flutter down with every flower that falls,
and worldly pleasures are tasteless as chewing wax.
My old grey head isn't has gone all brilliant white:
no good stirring up the monkey of the mind, the horse of the will.
I've planted my own marrows;
I gather my own tea leaves;
on the stove I boil my own elixirs:
I'll scan a volume of *The Way and its Power*,
chat a while with poachers or foresters,
in idleness shut the gate of my hibiscus hedge,
and lie drunk below my cucumber frame.
It's pure idleness altogether –
and I'm content beyond all measure!

Fine in Idleset

ti the air *Fankle o Jewelt Rammel*

ii

Nae bother, nae mishanter;
cannie hours at gloamin-faa amang the rowans an elms:
A niver let on ti play a hero's pairt,
tho ma pow's lyart wi aa yon fasherie A hed ti thole.

A've sleep galore
like the Halie Hermit on West Lily Hill,
tho nae Mensefu Monarch ever came
ti Whidderburn braes.
It isna at ma ettlin's aa turnt ti sweirtie:
A canna be daein wi wardlie gomerils an gowks.

Snaa haps the bens;
watter wimples about the annays;
fine A like the pickie-maas at plouter i the caum.

Sae be A ken *The Hornit Mune's Haas*,
A'm fleggit wi the *Lether ti the Cairrie*:
leukin that square i the face
still gets uis fair droukit wi sweit –

ochone for wearie men, whaur *Westlin Roads is Dour*!

玉交枝 • 閑適

Contented in Idleness

to the air *Tangle of Jade Branches*

二

無災無難
受用會桑榆日晚
英雄事業何時辦
空熬煎兩鬢斑
陳摶睡足西華山
文王不到磻溪岸
不是我心灰意懶
怎陪伴愚眉肉眼
雪滿山
水繞灘
靜愛野鷗閑
使見識偃月堂
受驚怕連雲棧
想起來滿面看
通身汗
慘煞人也蜀道難

2

No bother, no disasters;
comfortable hours at twilight among rowans[23] and elms:
a hero's part I never claimed to play,
but my temples are grey from the pointless troubles I had to suffer.
I have sleep in plenty, like the Holy Hermit on West Lily Hill,[24]
though the Cultured Monarch has never come to Whirling Stream's banks.[25]
It isn't that my ambition has all turned to laziness:
I have no patience with wordly fools and halfwits.
Snow covers the mountains;
water ripples round the river-islands;
I love the seagulls playing about in the stillness.
Even though I recognise the *The Horned Moon's Halls*,
I'm still frightened by the *Ladder to the Clouds*.
And when I think of looking these things full in the face,
I break out in a sweat.
Alas for miserable men, where *Western Roads are Hard*![26]

---

[23] Naturalised: *mulberry* in the original.
[24] The legendary Taoist sage Chen Tuan (871-989).
[25] The founder of the Zhou Dynasty, King Wen (1099–1050 BC), who met another hermit on this river.
[26] The song titles in italics have connotations to do with ambition and making a career.

Traivlin East-awa in the Year o 1336, Thinkin on the Past

ti the air *Poukin the Cannel*

Tír na nÓg;
auld trees,
lyart clouds,
an the corn
sae hie;
tod an cunnie
aa throuither
in ilka airt.

Heidstanes forhooiet,
burstit,
left;
auld larachs
i the tuim land,
aye an aa
gaen ti stour.

Wi the Hous o Easter Jin gaen doun,
anither Carrie Marischal
we're no like ti find;
wi braw Xi Shi awa,
the bonniest o weimen
we'll ne'er see mair.

Haar frae the sea,
a lang gloaming,
the dour skreichin
o yalla-yites.

In aa this warld,
There'll niver be anither spring.

折桂令・丙子游越懷古

Travelling in the East in the Year of 1336,
Thinking of the Past

to the air *Picking Cassia*

蓬萊老樹蒼雲
禾黍高低
孤兔紛紜
半折殘碑
空餘故址
總是黃塵
東晉亡也再難尋個右軍
西施去也絕不見甚佳人
海氣長昏
啼鴂聲干
天地無春

Tír na nÓg[27]; old trees, grizzled clouds,
and grain grown so high;
foxes and rabbits everywhere.
Headstones abandoned, broken, left;
old ruins in an empty land,
always and forever turning to dust.
With the House of Eastern Jin defunct,
another Marshal of the Left we're not likely to find;
with lovely Xi Shi gone, the rarest of women we'll see no more.
Mist off the sea, a long twilight, the dry screeching of shrikes.
In all this world, there'll never be another spring.

---

[27] Naturalised; *Penglai* in the original is the island paradise in the eastern seas; Tír na nÓg, the 'Land of Youth' in the Gaelic tradition, is the island paradise in the western seas.

Nae Titule

ti the air *Gaits on the Brae*

i

The clouds micht be dour or licht,
yir windae's mebbes derk or bricht:
nae guid snashin for the pearl in a bleck dragon's chafts.

It's gey fichly.
Dinna be grippy.
Mishantert wi the storm, ye'll be droukit bi the onding tae.
Whan watter's rinnin it's a dub: sae be it's tuim, it's aye a hole.

A gangin fuit?
A'll please masel.
Steyin pit?
A'll please masel.

山坡羊・失題

Untitled

to the air *Goats on the Hillside*

一
雲濃雲淡
窗明窗暗
等閑休擘驪龍頷
正尷尬
莫貪婪
惡風波吃閃的都著淹
流則盈科止則坎
行
也在俺
藏
也在俺

1

The clouds might be heavy or light,
your window might be dark or bright:
it's no good snatching at the pearl in a black dragon's jaws.
It's very tricky.
Don't be miserly.
Overtaken by the storm,
you'll be soaked by torrential rain.
When there's water running it's a pool,
if it's empty it's just a hole.
On the go?
I'll please myself.
Staying put?
I'll please myself.

Nae Titule

ti the air Gaits on the Brae

ii
Let on ye're daft, let on ye're a gowk;
let on ye're deif, let on ye're gyte gaen:
whit is't fowk are seekin aa their lifes?

Lilt a line in idletie,
tuim the gless fairly,
dream o white clouds about yir bowster i the green hills:
see them aa, the bonnie lassies, spreid about like braw brocade.

Happit wi glorie?
A'll think about it.
Dernt awa in hidlins?
A'll think about it.

山坡羊・失題

二

妝呆妝㑶
妝聾妝口吞
人生一世剛圖甚
句閑吟
酒頻斟
白雲夢繞青山枕
看遍洛陽花似錦
榮
也在恁
枯
也在恁

2
Pretend to be daft, pretend to be an idiot;
pretend you're deaf, pretend you've gone mad:
what is it people look for all their lives?
Sing a song in idleness,
drink off your glass,
dream of white clouds around your pillow in the green hills:
see the lovely girls spread out like fine brocade.
Covered in glory?
I'll think about it.
Hidden in obscurity?
I'll think about it.

Checkin Masel

ti the air Gaits on the Brae

Sittin idle in the caller air,
sleepin hie mang clouds of white:
nae leivin sowl gobs in ma gub!
A'll stot-stot in pleisur,
an lauch – haw haw!

See ither fowk,
yokit an shoved about,
worn doun ti the back-hauf,
aa ti mak a cantie wee bield.

East?
It's up ti me.
Wast?
It's up ti me.

山坡羊・自警

清風閑坐
白雲高臥
面皮不受時人唾
樂跎跎
笑呵呵
看別人搭套項推沈磨
蓋下一枚安樂窩
東
也在我
西
也在我

Reproving Myself

to the air *Goats on the Hillside*

Sitting idle in the fresh air,
sleeping high among white clouds,
no living soul spits in my face!
I'll stagger about merry,
and laugh, ha ha!
See others, harassed and bullied,
worn down to nothing, all to make a shelter.
East?
It's up to me.
West?
It's up to me.

The Warld Seen Throu

ti the air *The Flouer Lassie's Sang*

Ma hairt's been fired airn-hard
hunners o times:
walth an rank's a butterfly dwam
on midnicht's bowster.
Fame and gettin-on's unco
as an edder in yir quaich.
Snell wunds, fine snaa,
leavins i the pint-stoup, cauld kail –

the bricht lamp's smoorit
in ma bothy, inben its palins o bamboo.

賣花聲・悟世

肝腸百煉爐間鐵
富貴三更枕上蝶
功名兩字杯中蛇
尖風薄雪
殘杯冷炙
掩青燈竹籬茅舍

The World Seen Through

to the air *The Flower Girl's Song*

My heart has been forged iron-hard a hundred times:
wealth and rank a vain dream of a butterfly[28] on midnight's pillow,
success and fame unlikely as a snake in the wineglass.
Biting winds, fine snow,
leavings in the glass, cold cabbage –
the bright lamp is extinguished in my shack, behind its bamboo fence.

---

[28] Alluding to the philosopher Zhuangzi, who, after dreaming he was a butterfly one night, could never again be certain he wasn't a butterfly dreaming it was a philosopher.

The Eastren Palins
東籬

Ma Zhiyuan   (c.1250-1321)
馬致遠

Ma Zhiyuan, whose courtesy name 東籬 *Dongli* means *East Fence,* was a native of Beijing, and a one-time mandarin who is rated as possibly the greatest of the Mongol-era playwrights: his best-known work is the play *Autumn in the Palace of Han.* His later life was marked by a withdrawal from the world and a predilection for nature and poetry: the peace of the simple life in the country is a major theme of his later years, though he also wrote much about the carefree life of Taoist recluses and the spontaneous freedom of the Taoist Immortals, and his plays are notable for their pessimism about worldly ambition.

Critics with no sense of humour have long criticized him for being escapist and frivolous, while commending him for his exquisite style: he was also an innovator who greatly extended the range of subjects available to the poets of his day.

I the Haar, the Abbey's Gloamin Bell

ti the air *Vivific Sun*

寿陽曲・煙寺晚鐘

Cauld haar thins:
the auld abbey comes clear;
oncome o the derknin,
worshippers gie owre, are still.

Thrie-fower times on the westlin wind,
the jow o the evenin bell:
hou wad this gar a bit monk
set ti his meditation?

寒煙細
古寺清
近黃昏禮佛人靜
順西風晚鐘三四聲
怎生教僧禪定

In the Mist, the Abbey's Twilight Bell

to the air *Life-Giving Sun*

As the cold mist thins,
the old abbey appears.
With the coming of darkness, the worshippers cease, are still.
Three or four times on the western wind comes the tolling of the evening bell.
How would this make a monk sit down to his meditation?

壽陽曲 • 洞庭秋月

從別后
音信絕
薄情種害煞人也
逢一個見一個因話說
不信你耳輪兒不熱

Hairst Mune Owre Dongting Lochs

ti the air *Vivific Sun*

Yir letters stopt
efter we twa pairtit:
ye'll be the daith o me,
ye hairtless thing.

Whae'er ye meet, whae'er ye see
gets sweet naethins frae ye.
A hae nae douts –
yir lugs is burnin nou!

Autumn Moon Over Dongting Lakes

to the air *Life-Giving Sun*

After we parted
your letters stopped:
you'll be the death of me, you heartless thing.
You sweet-talk whoever you meet, whoever you see.
I have no doubts now – your ears are burning!

Hairst Time Wearyin

ti the air *Heaven's Undefylit Sauns*

i
withert vines
auld trees
derknin craws

wee brig
rinnin watter
bodies' houses

ancient road
westlin wind
shilpit jaud

gloamin sun
gaun westlins doun,
hairt sair, hairt sair
she's hauf the warld awa

ii
laich links
windlestraes
lyart an fauchie

sowff o burns
rinnin watters
tott-tottlin

on the border
caller hairst
early cauld

ae skreich
o new-come geese
yalla clouds, reid leafs, blae hills

iii
west wund
on the border
norlan flutes

bricht mune
on the pownie
a lute

sae it is
the Banisst Bride's
regrets wis monie

doun ablow
Rinagate's Law
pale rouks, dwynin gress, yalla sauns

天淨沙 · 秋思

Autumn Longings

to the air *Heaven's Pure Sands*

一

枯藤老樹昏鴉
小橋流水人家
古道西風瘦馬
夕陽西下
斷腸人在天涯

i

Withered creepers, old trees, twilight crows;
little bridge, flowing stream, folk's houses;
ancient road, western wind, skinny horse;
gloaming sun going down westward.
Heart sore, heart sore: she's half the world away.

二

平沙细草斑斑
曲溪流水潺潺
塞上清秋早寒
一声新雁
黄雲红叶青山

ii

Low-lying dunes, fine grass speckled and faded grey;
murmur of streams, babble of running water;
on the border clear autumn, early cold;
one cry of newly-arrived geese;
yellow clouds, red leaves, blue-grey hills.

三

西风塞上胡笳
明月马上琵琶
那底昭君恨多
李陵台下
淡烟衰草黄沙

iii

West wind on the border, northern flutes;
bright moon, a lute on the pony;
so it is, the Banished Bride's[29] regrets were many;
down below Renegade's Hill[30],
pale mist, withered grass, yellow sand.

---

[29] Wang Zhaojun, sent in 33BC as bride to the Hunnish Khan in the far north.

[30] General Li Ling (d.74BC) was the renegade: after suffering defeat in battle, he defected to the Huns. The Grand Historian Sima Qian suffered the punishment of judicial castration because he spoke up for Li Ling in 99BC.

In Praise o the Gillhaa Hills

歌頌廬山

The genesis of this selection of poems on the holy mountain of Lushan came in 2010, when the artist Alec Finlay asked me to translate some poems into English for *Lushan*, the section representing China in his project *Lushan–Schiehallion–Hiyori Yama–Arapaho Peaks: An Endless Word-Map Composed of Four Mountain Skylines*

Alec Finlay's word-map was produced for 'Poetic Forest', a sculpture-focused festival along the Yellow Dragon Temple Path, Mount Lushan, curated by Ute Ritschel. Four poets each contributed a poem, or translations, typeset in the form of a mountain skyline. The other contributors were Alec Finlay with *Schiehallion* (Scotland); Gerry Loose with *Hiyori-yama* (Japan), and Andrew Schelling with *Arapaho Peaks* (America).[16]

The final artwork was displayed on Mount Lushan in 2010. It consisted of a digital print of the word-map poem and two letterboxes containing rubber stamp circle poems by Alec Finlay.

In 2011, I re-translated some of these poems into Scots, dropping some and adding others. The name Lushan means Thatch-Roofed Hut Mountain.

---

[16] See http://china.waldkunst.com/en/artists-2010/alec-finlay Accessed 4th July 2013

Bai Juyi (772-846)

Fareweill Ti Ma Theikit Cot-hous

i

Doverin i the sun, A heard wee birds on the corrie,
on yalla paper, ma Letters Patent, lyin bi ma bowster;
A bude ti rise an cun ye thenks, ma lord, –
sae monie years gane by, ablow the Gillhaa Hills.

ii

Lang a solitar, in a rouch hodden plaid A sleepit,
but the justiciar's goun A maun put on, an be a baillie nou:
A'll hae ti quit ma theikit cot, but ma hairt'll bide on here,
an muckle mair, in years ti be, A'll scrieve about the Gillhaa Hills.

iii

Thrie wee theikit ruifs, forenenst the hills,
environit wi hill watters, they wir ma hame;
in sicht o the bens, hearin the burns, dowie wis A niver:
ma thrie year o duty dune, A'll be back here again.

白居易

別草堂三絕句

(一)
正聽山鳥向陽眠
黃紙除書落枕前
為感君恩須起
爐峰不擬住多年

(二)
久眠褐被為居士
忽掛緋袍作使君
身出草堂心不出
廬山未來動移文

(三)
三間茅舍向山開
一帶山泉繞舍回
山 色泉聲莫惆悵
三年官滿卻歸來

Bai Juyi

Farewell To My Thatched Cottage

i

I heard the little birds on the hill
as I was dozing in the sun;
my Letters Patent on yellow paper are lying by my pillow:
I ought to rise and give you thanks, my lord –
so many years have gone by,
below the peaks of Mount Lu.

ii

In a rough woollen blanket I slept,
so long a solitary,
but now I must put on the judge's robes
and be a mandarin:
I'll have to quit my thatched cottage,
but my heart will stay on here:
I'll write much more, in years to come,
about Mount Lu.

iii

Three little thatched roofs,
facing the mountains,
embraced by mountain streams –
this was my home.
In sight of the peaks, hearing the streams,
I was never sad at all.
My three years' duty done,
I'll be back here again.

127

Li Bai (701-762)

李白

Watchin the Linns mang the Gillhaa Hills

望廬山瀑布水

Wi the sun on the Incenser,
a purpie outher tovin rises,
as hyne awa the linn seems ti hing
frae the Foremaist Troch;
Doun it draps, birlin an brashin,
fair a thousan ells o't –
Ye'd think it wis the Milkmaid's Path,
faain throu the Ninefauld Lift!

日照香爐生紫煙
遙看瀑布掛前川
飛流直下三千尺
疑是銀河落九天

Watching the Falls of Mt. Lu

With the sun on the Censer,
a purple haze billows up,
as far away the falls seem to hang
from the Forward Trough;
the water drops, spinning and battering down,
easily a thousand yards of it –
you'd think it was the Milky Way
falling through the Nine Layers of Heaven!

李 白   Li Bai   (701-762)

望廬山五老峰   *Viewin the Five Bodachs o the Gillhaa Hills*

廬山東南五老峰   The peaks o the Five Bodachs
青天削出金芙蓉   lies south-east o the Gillhaa Hills,
九江秀色可攬結   whaur the blue lift's cut
吾將此地巢雲松   wi the gowden roses o hairst;
                              Aa Nineburn's bonnie sichts
                                lies in atween ma airms:
                            In amang the clouds an pines,
                                it's here A'll big ma nest.

                         Viewing the Five Old Men of Mt. Lu

                        The peaks of the Five Old Men lie
                               east of Mount Lu,
                           where the blue sky is cut
                        with the golden roses of autumn;
                        the lovely sights of Nine Streams
                             lie in my arms, each one.
                        In among the clouds and pines,
                        this is where I'll build my nest.

Yuan Zhen   779-831   元 積

A Lanesome Nicht on the Gillhaa Hills

A Lanesome Nicht on the Gillhaa Hills   廬 山 獨 夜

Cauld's the lift, an snaa's on the Five Bodachs;
doun sklents the mune, an owre Nineburns there's clouds.
The jow o thon bell – whaur's it comin frae?
It's dirlin throu auld foggie wuids.

寒空五老雪
斜月九江雲
鐘聲知何處
蒼蒼樹里聞

A Lonely Night on Mt. Lu

The sky is cold, and there's snow on the Five Old Men;
the moon slants down, and there are clouds over the Nine Streams.
The toll of that bell – where is it coming from?
It's ringing through old mossy woods.

白居易 　　　　　　　　　　 Bai Juyi　772-846

大林寺桃花

人間四月芳菲盡
山寺桃花始盛開
長恨春歸無覓處
不知轉入此中來

Peach-Flourish at Meiklewuid Tempill

The simmer's douce flourish is by nou,
doun i the warld o men,
but the peach flouers is juist out
at this fane in the hills;
hairt-sair A wis at Spring wis gane,
wi no a haet left ahint:
but Spring flittit awa up here –
hou did A niver ken?

Peach-Blossom at Micklewood Temple

The summer's sweet burgeoning is now past
down in the world of men,
but the peach blossom is just out
at this holy place in the hills.
I was heart-broken that Spring had gone,
and left not a thing behind.
But Spring had moved up here –
so how did I never know?

Li Qi   ?690-?751

Stoppin i the Broch at Dulcehill Tempill

Haufroads up the verdant braes aa nicht A lay,
an heard the derk burn faa owre the Hie Binks,
wi farawa lamps cairriet on outbye cobles,
an the canny waff o hill airs.
Ma jaiket skifft at pinetrees in the cairrie,
ma yett wis hingin outowre the Milky Way,
bens an ballochs taiglt owre ma bowster:
the warlds o men an gods cleikit thegither.
Misty rooks rase frae grushie lees,
scarrows o sternies skinklt on the water.
In deep wuids fu o simmer's wheelie-oes,
wearie, wae, A cudna speak, sae hame-awa A turnt.

李頎

宿香山寺石樓

夜宿翠微半
高檔聞暗泉
漁舟帶遠火
山馨發孤煙
衣拂雲松外
門清河漢邊
峰巒依枕席
世界接人天
藹藹花出霧
輝輝星映川
深林暑鶯滿
惆悵欲言還

Li Qi

Spending the Night in the Tower of Dulcehill Temple

I lay all night halfway up the green slope,
and heard the dark streams fall over the High Shelves,
with the faraway lamps carried by the skiffs away out there,
and the cheery scent of hill air.
My jacket brushed against pine trees in the clouds,
and my door hung out over the Milky Way.
Mountains and high passes crowded over my pillow,
the world of men and the world of gods conjoined.
Mists and fogs rose from luxuriant meadows,
and stars' reflections were still glittering on the water.
In deep woods full of summer's willow-warblers,
weary, miserable, I couldn't speak, so turned for home.

Wang Wei   (699-759)   王維

Brither Hyneawa's Sanctuarie   遠公龕

The back road throu the pines leads ti a closter,
a blossom-bussed sanctuarie at minds an auld monk.
A lean on ma staff mang laithron clouds,
while in gowden flauchts the sun gaes doun.
Whan nicht hes faan owre the derk brae-faces,
mang a thousan bens, the ae licht'll aye be leamin.

松路向精舍
花龕歸老僧
閑雲撥錫杖
落日低金繩
入夜翠微里
千峰明一燈

Brother Faraway's Sanctuary

The back road through the pines leads to a cloister,
a flower-bedecked sanctuary that commemorates an old monk.
I lean on my staff amid the lazy clouds,
while the sun goes down in golden flame.
When night has fallen over the dark hillsides,
among a thousand mountains, that one light will always be burning.

徐凝

廬 山 瀑 布

The Linn o the Gillhaa Hills

瀑布瀑布千丈直
雷奔入海不息
今古長如白練飛
一條界破青山色

The linn, the linn, it draps
a thousan ells strecht doun,
bullerin awa ti the sea
wi nae devaul;
frae auld langsyne,
like siller soy outowre the lift,
an aefauld line at's aye spylt the look
o thae green green hills.

The Waterfall on Mt. Lu

The waterfall, the waterfall, it drops a thousand yards straight down,
its waters boiling away toward the sea, without a pause.
Since times long past, like silver silk spread out across the sky,
a single line that's always spoiled the look of these green, green hills.

Du Mu   (802-853)

On the Eastwuid Tempill Path on the Gillhaa Hills

A ferlie interpells ma dottlin eild
amang the suddron watters,
Wi the firsten reid of faain leafs,
the back-en o this year;
thrang's the Toun's wynds,
whaur it's ill to fin a meinit's peace,
tho verdant hills hes aye been there,
wi easedom ti the een.
A've snowkit eftir rank an pelf,
an hie estait in the nation,
niver sat in the Tuim Hous,
nor leirit meditation;
gin A wis learnt ti saunt awa,
like the Senatour, in years ti be,
A whiles wad hae ti come richt back
ti thir five lochans sae drowie.

杜牧

行經廬山東林寺

離魂斷續楚江氒
葉墜初紅十月天
紫陌事多難暫息
青山長在好閑眼
方趨上國期干祿
未得空堂學坐禪
他歲若教為范蠡
也應須入五湖煙

Du Mu

On the Eastwood Temple Path on Mt. Lu

A wonder interrupts my tottering old age
among these southern waters;
with the first red of falling leaves,
comes the autumn of the year.
The city's lanes are thronged,
and it's hard to find a minute's peace,
though the verdant hills have always been here,
bringing ease to the eye.
I've sneaked about after rank and gold,
and a high place in the state,
but never sat in the Empty House
nor learned to meditate.
Even if in years to come, like the Senator,[17]
I was taught to vanish away,
I'd still have to come back sometimes
to these five little drizzly lakes.

[17] Fan Li, fl. 473BC, an influential statesman who became an immortal, and lived on the lakes with the loveliest woman of the age.

Wang Zhenbai (875-?)

王貞白

White Hart Weems

白鹿洞

A niver seen, as A conned ma quair,
 hou fer the Spring hed gaed,
 ilka inch o the sun's flauchts,
 an inch o leamin gowd:
 it wisna your comin, Sir,
 at brocht the smile ti ma face,
but juist masel, ettlin ti be wyce,
 an mensefu, an guid.

讀書不覺已春深
一寸光陰一寸金
不是道人來引笑
周情孔思正追尋

White Hart Grottoes

I didn't see, as I carefully read my book,
 how far the Spring had come,
 with every inch of the sun's rays
 an inch of shining gold.
 It wasn't your coming, Sir,
 that made me smile,
but just me, always trying to be wise,
 and sensible, and good.

Afterword

I was born at 11.45 a.m. on Monday 11th July 1949, the first of fraternal twin brothers, in the Cottage Hospital at Netherdale in Galashiels, while my parents were on leave from Nigeria. My father Cyril Holton was the sixth of seven children, the youngest son of a family which moved from Waterford to Liverpool at the end of the First World War; his father and his uncle were both engineers with the Ben Line, sailing to Hong Kong, Canton, Shanghai and Yokohama, as were two of my mother's uncles, Alec Young and Alec Smith.

Dad was sent off to boarding school at an early age to be educated in French, and was bilingual. After a parachute accident in Egypt (he was a commando, and had fought in the Western Desert) he spent several months recuperating in Tanganyika, where he learned Swahili, adding it to the Latin and Greek he had learned in the seminary; after his medical discharge in 1943, he married my mother Isobel Young, who he had met while on an army training course in Galashiels, and he found a job in northern Nigeria which required him to learn Hausa as soon as possible. After my brother Harvey and I were born, we moved to Lagos, where Dad added Yoruba to his languages, although the working language at home was mostly West African Pidgin, in which Mum, a natural Border Scots speaker, was also competent. When my brother Norman was born in 1951, Harvey and I had already been given the Hausa names of Hassan and Hussein, first twin and second twin: so Norman was Gambo, the child born after twins.

At an early age, I was accustomed to a multilingual environment: our houseboy Dennis Oziri told us bedtime stories in Pidgin, and Uncle Ali, a Hausa trader and old friend of my parents, was a favourite visitor we loved to play with, though he spoke no English, while our lullabies and bairn-rhymes were mostly in Scots.

We came home to Edinburgh to start school in 1954, and never went back to West Africa, though my father stayed on for a year or so. Scotland in the fifties, still in the grip of postwar austerity, was a dourer, drabber place than it is now, and Lagos, for Harvey and me, became a memory of a prelapsarian paradise, an Eden in that big house at 26 Point Road, Apapa, which had an orchard in its compound, deadly snakes in the flowerbeds, scarlet and gold military bands marching in and out of the army barracks at the end of the road, and, as we went to sleep under our mosquito nets, the jazzy sound of High Life music drifting over from the night club in the street behind us.

Dad used to play language games with us, especially at mealtimes, when we had to ask for what we wanted in the language of his choice – Hausa, Yoruba, Swahili, and so on. Shortly before he died, Norman told me that he could still remember the Swahili for sugar, and the Hausa for salt. My grandfather Samuel MacDiarmid Young – a cousin of Hugh MacDiarmid – took a great interest in our development, and had us playing memory games like Pelmanism or Kim's Game.

Later, I began Latin and French at Larbert High School, then, at Galashiels Academy, I was extremely fortunate to study under three excellent teachers: I began Greek and continued with Latin under Donald Gibson, continued French under the inspiring and demanding Mysie Hargreaves, and read for Higher English under Donald McInnes, a Skye man who, uniquely for that time, gave equal weight to literature in both Scots and English. We read from the mediaeval Makars, Henryson, Dunbar, and Gawain Douglas, through the Border Ballads, on to Stevenson, Scott and Hogg, and right up to the writers of the twentieth-century Scottish Renaissance, such as Hugh MacDiarmid, Sydney Goodsir Smith, and Lewis Grassic Gibbon. In the then state-of-the art language lab I taught myself a little German, and in my final year I had the opportunity to learn a little Russian.

And there you have it: how could I not be a translator?

Chinese came to me through Gala Academy library. I had been reading Arthur Waley's *The Opium War Through Chinese Eyes* with both a burning sense of injustice that this history had not been taught in school, and a dawning realization of how and why the Chinese and Japanese bric-à-brac that I had unthinkingly grown up with had come to be in my grandfather's house. As I replaced the book on the shelf, though, I noticed a slim volume: Arthur Waley's *100 Chinese Poems*. I was daft about poetry, reading as much as I possibly could in any of the languages I had access to, but that *coup de foudre* seems as sharp to me now as it was that day in 1965: it had never occurred to me that Chinese people would write poetry. As I devoured Waley, followed it with Pound's *Cathay*, then borrowed the frustratingly uncooperative *Teach Yourself Chinese* from the public library, I felt tantalizingly close to something big, knowing I needed to know more, but not knowing where to go next. Then, later in my fifth year, as I was preparing to apply to university, I noticed a paragraph in the *Scotsman* announcing that Edinburgh University was to begin a degree course in Chinese Studies, and, against much advice from some of my teachers and some of my family, I decided to apply.

After a false start in 1967-9, I went back in 1971 to study under John Chinnery, Dou Daoming, the inspirational and impossible John Scott, and the erudite and delightful William Dolby, and I graduated *summa cum laude* in 1975. In 1976-8 I read for a PhD (never completed) at Durham University; then, since my exit from my studies coincided with Nigel Lawson and Margaret Thatcher's experiment with the British economy, I entered a period of unemployment or short-term work, which gave me time to experiment with translations from the Chinese.

But why Scots? Well, why not? It's one of my mother tongues, after all.[1]

It came to me in one summer evening in 1965, as I was standing outside Joe's Café in Selkirk Market Place with Cathy Cockburn. A Selkirk lad came by and said to her, "Ir oo aa gaun soomin at the Skerrs the morn's morn?" (Are we all going swimming at the cliffs tomorrow morning?). It was a revelation: I had begun to see the Latin roots of French and grasp the relationship between Greek and Latin, and I suddenly understood that what I had just heard – the tongue that I spoke among my school friends and with much of my mother's family – wasn't the 'bad English' primary school teachers had proscribed, or any sort of 'slang', but a language in its own right, separate to and distinct from English. Donald McInnes's lessons had sunk in, so I set myself to read as much of the literature in Scots as I could, and to spend more time listening to my Galashiels-born grandmother and her peers.

At this same time, my twin brother Harvey began to take an interest in Scots, publishing his first poems in 1966 or 1967. Scots became his chosen medium, and after graduating from Dundee University, where he immersed himself in the literatures of Scotland, he began to publish highly original and carefully crafted poetry, and became a well-regarded poet whose work is now seen as pivotal to the development of the next generation of Dundee and Fife poets. He settled in North Fife in his undergraduate years, and spent the rest of his life there, a respected and much-loved teacher of writing, though he insisted he was happy to be seen as a local bard who provided poems for weddings, christenings, anniversaries and such. His example, and his finely-wrought and metrically intricate work, were always an inspiration to me: he showed me how to turn my translations into living poems, and I honour his memory for that, as for much else. *Forsan et haec olim meminisse iuvabit.*

---

[1] I refer readers who don't know Scots to the magisterial *Dictionar o the Scots Leid* (*Dictionary of the Scots Language*) at www.dsl.ac.uk where they will find an introduction to what RL Stevenson called 'this elegant and malleable tongue'.

The impulse to translate into Scots came in 1980. As an undergraduate, I had been unable to visit China because of the chaos of the so-called Cultural Revolution, and had spent much of the four years of my MA course reading. In my honours years of 1973-1975 I specialized in pre-modern fiction and drama, which we read *in extenso*, though we also read much poetry too, and my favourite book was *Shuihu Zhuan*[2]. I adored the book, but found the English versions very poor indeed, and began to feel that I could do better. I tried in English, but it was stiff and unresponsive to the needs of a mediaeval outlaw novel, the first masterpiece of vernacular Chinese, and a book whose language is fresh, new-made, flexible and innovative. One evening in our cottage in Gattonside, I was explaining this to my first wife, Monika Dunlop, and she said, "Well, you've spent the last few years reading all you can find in Scots, so why don't you try it in Scots?" I demurred: I had never been taught to write Scots, had never written it, didn't know if I could, and so on. But the next day I sat down at the typewriter, and the first few paragraphs just fell on to the page. I hadn't known I could do this, and the match with the vibrant colloquial language of the original was so neat, I was amazed and delighted by it. When I had finished the first chapter, I sent copies of my second draft to John Scott and Bill Dolby. Bill, who translated Chinese into Welsh, was so excited, he rushed down Buccleuch Place to the office of the literary quarterly *Cencrastus*, whose editor Glenn Murray immediately agreed to serialise my translation. I was off![3]

Some poems in this book were done in the early eighties, as test-pieces to see if I could make classical Chinese poetry work in Scots. Some were commissioned, but most were done for the sheer joy of it. Some have been revised again and again over the years, some have been specially revised for this book, and some have been translated here for the first time. *Staunin Ma Lane* isn't intended to be a comprehensive tour of classical poetry, though it does contain specimens of many of the major genres and styles, and it may serve as a first primer. Note that the poetry is in the Scots: the English versions are there to help the non-Scots speaker. It has been my aim to make poems in Scots: if you expect to find dictionary definitions of Chinese words in my translations, you will be disappointed. That sort of drably mechanical 'accuracy' does not make poetry, and a poem that doesn't move the reader is like a joke that isn't funny. In the translation of poetry, there are many, many more ways of being wrong than of being right, and I do not claim that my versions are in any

---

[2] Known as *The Water Margin*, *All Men Are Brothers*, or *Outlaws of the Marshes* in its various English translations.

[3] Though some chapters of my *Men o the Mossflow* appeared in *Cencrastus* and in *The Edinburgh Review* under Peter Kravitz, no publisher has so far seen fit to publish more of it. A sample may be found at http://tentietranslations. weebly.com/work-mossflow.html

way definitive or better than anyone else's: I do, however, want to say to the reader, "Deek whit the Mither Tongue can dae: gin it can dae this, whit'll it no can dae?" (Look what our mother tongue can do: if it can do this, what will it not do?), and I would urge readers inclined toward translation to do it for themselves, whatever their mother tongue might be. I may be the only Chinese-Scots translator in captivity, but I wouldn't half welcome some company.

So I present you here, reader, with some of the fruits of a lifetime of happy translating. See what can happen when you pick a book from a library shelf?

An gin ye're eftir onie mair, here's this:

Pi Rixiu

皮 日 休

c.834-883

The Spring o Mense

聪 明 泉

The ae an ane ladlefu's the watter o life itsel,
    an it'll mak a saunct o a gomeril:
      ye're the better for't, think ye?
Or wis it Gundie-Guts Well ye drank frae?

一勺如瓊液
將愚擬聖賢
欲知心不變
還似飲貪泉

The Spring of Good Sense

Just one ladleful is the water of life itself,
And it will make a saint of an idiot.
Are you any the better for it, do you think?
Or was it Greedy-Guts Well you drank from?

Brian Holton
Melrose, July 2015

144

Lightning Source UK Ltd.
Milton Keynes UK
UKOW05f2334011117
312001UK00002B/4/P